T0222254

Apple Watch for Developers

Advice & Techniques from Five
Top Professionals

Gary Riches
Ruben Martinez Jr.
Jamie Maison
Matt Klosterman
Mark Griffin

Apress®

Apple Watch for Developers: Advice & Techniques from Five Top Professionals

ISBN-13 (pbk): 978-1-4842-1339-1

ISBN-13 (electronic): 978-1-4842-1338-4

Managing Director: Welmoed Spahr

Lead Editor: Steve Weiss

Technical Reviewer: Iliya Yordanov

Editorial Board: Steve Anglin, Gary Cornell, Louise Corrigan, James T. DeWolf, Jonathan Gennick, Robert Hutchinson, Michelle Lowman, James Markham, Matthew Moodie, Jeffrey Pepper, Douglas Pundick, Ben Renow-Clarke, Gwenan Spearing, Matt Wade, Steve Weiss

Coordinating Editor: Kevin Walter

Project Editor: Troy Mott

Copy Editor: Christina Rudloff

Cover Designer: Crest

Distributed to the book trade worldwide by Springer Science+Business Media New York, 233 Spring Street, 6th Floor, New York, NY 10013. Phone 1-800-SPRINGER, fax (201) 348-4505, e-mail orders-ny@springer-sbm.com, or visit www.springeronline.com. Apress Media, LLC is a California LLC and the sole member (owner) is Springer Science + Business Media Finance Inc (SSBM Finance Inc). SSBM Finance Inc is a Delaware corporation.

For information on translations, please e-mail rights@apress.com, or visit www.apress.com.

Apress and friends of ED books may be purchased in bulk for academic, corporate, or promotional use. eBook versions and licenses are also available for most titles. For more information, reference our Special Bulk Sales–eBook Licensing web page at www.apress.com/bulk-sales.

Any source code or other supplementary materials referenced by the author in this text is available to readers at www.apress.com. For detailed information about how to locate your book's source code, go to www.apress.com/source-code/.

Contents at a Glance

Contents

Preface

This book is for developers who already have a basic knowledge of developing with WatchKit and watchOS 2, and who are now interested in learning how to use them to create cutting-edge Watch apps. It is written by five experienced Apple Watch developers who have created their own apps early on, and will now show you how to best create your own Apple Watch apps.

The examples in this book use Objective-C and Swift version 1.2 and were tested with Xcode 6.3 and 6.4.

If you are just starting out in this space, be sure to pick up and read the Apress beginner's book for Apple Watch development, "Learn WatchKit for iOS." If you have already read that, or have already gotten your feet wet, then this book is for you.

About the Authors

Gary Riches is a longstanding member of the iOS developer community and is the founder of Bouncing Ball, where he develops high quality iOS applications and games incorporating augmented reality, multiplayer, bluetooth communication, and interfacing with hardware peripherals. Forbes profiled Riches as having developed one of the "most anticipated Apple Watch Apps."

Ruben Martinez Jr. is a student at Bowdoin College, where he studies Computer Science and Visual Arts with the goal of learning to build products that can improve people's lives. He has led a student group that uses technology to improve student life, and has built several iOS, Android, and web applications for students. He also started the first student hackathon in Maine, CBBhacks. During his free time, Ruben founded a social-discovery startup for connecting people with similar interests, built a fully-responsive web and mobile application for a medical startup, and is currently developing three apps for the iPhone: Infinitweet, Twindr, and TouchLocker.

Matt Klosterman hails from Dallas, TX and is an iOS and Apple Watch app developer at Infofission LLC. Klosterman got his first taste of mobile development in 2004 working with real-time weather data. He released his first iOS app in 2008 and since 2010 has focused on mobile consulting projects for Fortune 500 companies.

Jamie Maison is a British software engineer, specialising in iOS development and UI/UX design using Objective-c and Swift. After graduating from the University of Kent with a degree in Music Technology he founded Notation, an iOS app that converts audio to musical score and guitar tablature. Jamie is an advocate for utilizing the best practices in software development, focusing on performance, usability and function. He can be found at http://www.jamiemaison.com and on twitter @jamiemaison

Mark Griffin has been developing various applications across a number of devices and platforms including web, mobile, wearable and interactive digital outdoor installations. He has been involved in many cutting edge campaigns and picked up many prestigious awards along the way including Golden Cannes Cyber Lions and D&AD Pencils.

About the Technical Reviewer

Iliya Yordanov is the founder and CEO of SilverWiz, a company that is building a portfolio of premium productivity applications. His application, MileWiz, was named one of the hottest Apple Watch apps from an independent developer this year by Wearable.com.

Acknowledgments

Thanks to my wife, Sophie, for putting up with all the long hours, to my daughter, Evie, for my allowing my constant trips to the study, and the bump for giving me the drive and determination to keep on developing.

—*Gary Riches*

"To my friend Kaylee, who always had to write more than I did.

—*Ruben Martinez*

For my wife, Shaila, and my children, Madison, Jack, and Luke. Thank you for all of your extra effort and understanding while I spent months away from home to pursue a dream.

—*Matt Klosterman*

Chapter 1

An Apple Watch Introduction

Back in September of 2014, Apple announced their first new product line since the iPad in 2010. In an unusual move for Apple, they gave developers access to the Apple Watch SDK, and the public information on a device that wasn't to ship for another seven months. The delay between announcement and release was important because although it was most likely production issues that caused the delay, the Apple Watch presents a new paradigm with different user interaction methods, and usage levels measured in seconds rather than minutes. Developers were able to start building apps for the Apple Watch with the SDK that Apple provided and quickly realized that the traditional ways of planning and building iOS apps wouldn't directly translate to the Apple Watch, so the time would be required to get a feel for what works and what doesn't.

The Apple Watch still has touch input, but also a mechanical way of scrolling with the Digital Crown and a new technology called Force Touch, which is able to detect varying levels of pressure on the Watch's screen. Some of the new technologies present are not accessible via Apple's APIs yet, and in general WatchKit, Apple's name for the Apple Watch-specific code, is a very cut down version of what it will eventually be. This is most likely to preserve battery on the Apple Watch, but the limitations should be embraced. The skills you will learn with WatchKit in terms of app optimization can be moved back up into your iOS app development process.

By now you should hopefully have your Apple Watch devices because the opportunity to test on real hardware is invaluable. If, however, you don't, then do what you can to simulate the Watch. There are some great paper templates available that you can print out and use, or apps such as WatchSim by Danny Keogan, which allow you to see a 1:1 image of the Watch on your iPhone that mirrors the Apple Watch simulator. Indeed, sometimes it's faster to do it this way rather than deploying to real hardware each time.

Along with every major new Apple iOS or hardware release is the opportunity to be first to market, to capture the eyes of users eager to test the features of the new iOS, or to download apps that exploit the new device's features. The Apple Watch is going to be "new" for a good while yet, and the amount of apps currently in the App Store with Apple Watch support is a fraction of that in the main iOS App Store. All of these factors together mean that you'll hopefully find more success, since there is a smaller pool of apps to choose from. It will be easier to be the best.

Let's look at the structure of an Xcode project to see what Xcode creates, where it gets created, and why.

> **Note** For Apple watchOS 2 the extension runs on the Apple Watch instead of the iOS device, and App Groups no longer work. Home Remote was written with Watch OS 1, and given that the feature list of watchOS 2 is not yet fully defined, we'll be using Watch OS 1 for the example here.

Anatomy of a WatchKit App

A WatchKit app is always bolted on to an existing iOS project, it's just a different target. It has two distinct parts: the WatchKit extension and the WatchKit app, and they are both bundled within the iOS app. The WatchKit extension remains on your iOS device and does the work while the WatchKit app is copied to the Watch's internal storage along with the storyboard and any images or assets you included in the WatchKit app extension.

Your WatchKit app storyboard can contain any of three different types of controllers, and they are: Interface Controllers, Glance Interface Controllers, and Notification Interface Controllers. Let's look at these controllers one by one.

The Interface Controller

A single interface controller object manages each scene, which is an instance of the WKInterfaceController class. A WatchKit interface controller performs the same tasks as a view controller in iOS, it will present and manage content that is displayed on the screen, and it handles user interactions with the on-screen content. However, unlike a view controller, an interface controller doesn't manage the actual views of your interface-- all of that is handled for you behind the scenes by WatchKit. This is nice in the respect that it's very simple to put a scene together quickly, but can make creating scenes more difficult if the layout you want doesn't fit in to the restrictions placed upon WatchKit apps.

WatchKit apps typically contain multiple interface controllers, with each one displaying some different information. The interface is primarily user input driven, in so much that a new interface controller is typically presented after the user has interacted with the screen or a button.

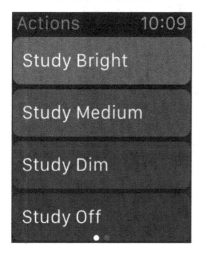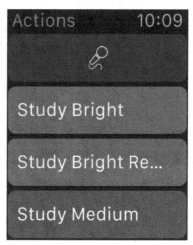

Figure 1.1. The interface of a WatchKit app

Glance Interfaces

A glance is a window into your app and should display an app's most pertinent information. Glances are named as such because they're intended to be looked at quickly by the user. They're not made to scroll; the entire glance interface must fit on a single screen and they cannot contain buttons, switches, or other interactive controls. Xcode will throw an error if you do anything illegal with a glance. Glances appear when you swipe up from your Watch face, which means they are a quick and easy way to see part or all of your app. Tapping a glance launches your WatchKit app.

Even with all of the restrictions Apple places on glances, they are incredibly useful as a shortcut in to the app, even though Apple says you shouldn't create one solely for this purpose. You can only have one glance in your storyboard, but you can configure the information it displays based on context such as location, time of day, or user settings.

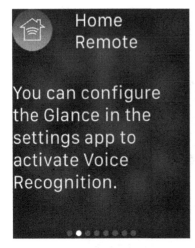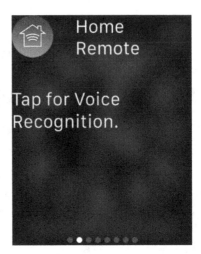

Figure 1.2. The Home Remote configurable Glance interface

Notification Interfaces

The Apple Watch works with its paired iOS device to display local and remote notifications. By default, the Apple Watch uses a minimal interface to display incoming notifications. The user will receive Taptic feedback and upon raising their wrist they will see a very brief snippet of information. If the user holds their arm in place so that the display stays on, the minimal interface changes to a more detailed interface displaying the contents of the notification. This detailed interface is customizable and you can add your own graphics or arrange the notification data differently from the default interface provided by the system.

The Apple Watch notification system has support for the actionable notifications introduced in iOS 8 with no need for any extra work to implement. Actionable notifications are a way to add buttons to your notification interface that reflect the actions the user could take. For example, a notification for a Tweet directed at you might include buttons to reply, retweet, or favorite a tweet. When your iOS app registers support for actionable notifications, the Apple Watch automatically adds appropriate buttons to the notification interfaces on the Apple Watch. All you need to do is handle the actions that the user selects. You do this in your WatchKit extension.

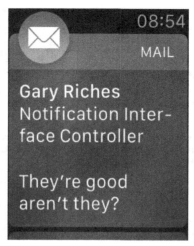

Figure 1.3. An example of Notifications on the Apple Watch

Interface Navigation

If your WatchKit app has more than one screen of content, you'll need to work out which navigation type is the best fit. There are two types of navigation for WatchKit apps; you can use either one or the other, but not both.

- *Page based.* This style of navigation is best suited for apps with a simple flow where the data on each page isn't too closely related to the data on any other page, or the app flow is very linear: you will always perform A, followed by B, followed by C. It needs to contain two or more independent interface controllers, and only one of those is displayed at any given time. At runtime, the user navigates between interface controllers by swiping left or right on the screen. A pagination indicator control at the bottom of the screen indicates the user's current position among the pages. If you're having trouble visualizing this, it's very similar to the home screen on iOS, the one with all of your apps. The list of glances accessible from the Watch face screen is a good example of page based navigation.

Figure 1.4. The dots at the bottom indicate this is a page based navigation

- *Hierarchical.* This style of navigation is suited for apps with more closely related screens of information or apps whose data is more hierarchical. The hierarchical interface always starts with a single root interface controller, which provides controls that, when pressed, will push related interface controllers on to the screen showing more detailed information. The Photos app on iOS is a good example of this, with screens of years, collections, and moments, all relating to one another. The Settings app on the Apple Watch is another good example of hierarchical navigation.

Figure 1.5. A hierarchical navigation example can be seen in the Settings app

Although you cannot mix page based and hierarchical navigation styles in your app, you can present other interface controllers above the one currently displayed by using modal presentations. Modal presentations will interrupt the current user workflow and display information or choices to the user. You can present interface controllers modally from both page based and hierarchical apps. The modal presentation itself can be a single screen, or multiple screens arranged in a page based layout, although if you're going to go this route you should maybe see if it can be achieved in a more intuitive way.

Context Menus

The Retina display on the Apple Watch features a new technology called Force Touch, and provides a new way to interact with content. Previously, you only had a press or a long press available, but now, pressing the screen with a small amount of force activates the context menu if there is one associated with the current interface controller. Context menus are optional but they are a great way to add common controls, or you can use them to display actions related to the current screen. WatchKit displays the menu over your content.

A context menu can display up to four actions, along with a title string and an image to represent each action. Tapping an action's image dismisses the menu and runs the action method associated with that menu item. Tapping anywhere else dismisses the menu without any further action.

Summary

That's the basics. Hopefully now you'll understand a little about how a watch app is structured, the types of screens you can have, and how to move through them all. We'll cover most of the things mentioned here in greater detail through the following chapters. Next up, we're going to look at one of the major components in WatchKit, the WKInterfaceTable, which is the WatchKit version of the UITableView.

Chapter 2

Examining the Stopwatch, Timer and Calendar

By Jamie Maison, creator of the Notation Watch app

When the Apple Watch was announced, it became clear that the device's strengths would be in its quick, simple and functional applications. Users were not going to want to spend a large amount of time on their watches and would instead rely on it as a device that provides a quicker way of receiving notifications and performing functions.

With this is mind, this chapter seeks to explore three types of applications that the Apple Watch will be successful for: the stopwatch, timer, and calendar. Each of these applications provides quick functionality while remaining entirely useful to the user.

The best Apple Watch applications will perform functions that take very few taps of a button. This chapter explains how these interactions are handled while exploring the code behind timing something as accurately and as efficiently as possible.

We will also look at how users can program push notifications into their applications much like the calendar application while using iCloud to send data back and forth. iCloud is an essential part of application development on iOS these days, and this chapter will help you by teaching you the fundamentals of using iCloud with the Apple Watch.

Stopwatch

In this tutorial we will create a simple stopwatch application that has a label for displaying our time, a start button to trigger the function to begin timing, and a Lap button that will allow us to record our lap times. We will look at the best practice for timing using Objective-C to the most precise value possible that the Apple Watch can process. We will be creating this as a native watchOS app because the Apple Watch can easily handle the processing we will be implementing.

Creating the User Interface

The very first step that we have to take is to create the user interface, which will consist of three elements, a label, and two actions. To do this on the Apple Watch the fist step is to simply head over to your Interface.storyboard within your watchOS application and add a label from the object library. We may want to center the label to make our application look a little more aesthetic. To do this we simply head over to our Attributes Inspector and set the horizontal position to Center. Next we want to change the text of the label to say 00:00.00. This is merely a placeholder text to indicate that our timer has yet to begin timing.

The next step is to add two buttons that will sit side-by-side of each other. To do this we need to add a Group by selecting the group object from the Object Library and placing it underneath our label. Next we add two buttons and place them side-by-side. You may notice that one of the buttons is not yet visible and the first button is taking up 100 percent of the width of the screen. To remedy this, simply head over to the Attributes Inspector and set the width of each button to 0.5. Finally, name one button START, and the other LAP.

Later on we will also be creating a table to store and handle all of the lap results, but for now your user interface should look like what is shown in Figure 2.1.

Figure 2.1. Starting our user interface

Outlets and Actions

The next step we have to take is to link these elements within our application. The best way to do this is to open the Assistant Editor by clicking the icon in the top right hand corner of Xcode. This way we can create our IBOutlet and IBActions for our label, and buttons by simply control clicking the element in our user interface and dragging it over to our .h file. We want to create an IBOutlet for our label and call it timeLabel, two IBActions for our buttons called startTime and lapTime. Your InterfaceController.h file should now look like this.

```
#import <WatchKit/WatchKit.h>
#import <Foundation/Foundation.h>

@interface InterfaceController : WKInterfaceController
@property (weak, nonatomic) IBOutlet WKInterfaceLabel *timeLabel;
- (IBAction)startTime;
- (IBAction)lapTime;
@end
```

Here we can see that we have declared three things, an outlet for our label and our two actions. We are now ready to start coding the timing part of our application!

We need to add two extra properties to our InterfaceController.h file as follows.

```
@property (strong, nonatomic) NSTimer *watchTimer;
@property (strong, nonatomic) NSDate *startDate;
```

These two properties will store the time and date so that we can later use these to produce our accurate time.

Triggering Timing

The next step is to head over to our .m file to implement the code that will actually keep time on our Apple Watch application. Firstly, we want to create a method that will do our processing, which we will call updateTimer. Within this method we first want to save the time each time the method is fired. To do this we use the NSDate startDate that we created earlier.

```
NSDate *dateNow = [NSDate date];
NSTimeInterval interval = [dateNow timeIntervalSinceDate:self.startDate];
NSDate *timeDate = [NSDate dateWithTimeIntervalSince1970:interval];
```

Next we want to format this time into something that is easily readable and useful for our users. I recommend formatting the time in hours, minutes and seconds because it will look a whole lot better than cramming milliseconds into our user interface for little gain. To do this we use NSDateFormatter and tell it to process the time in the format HH:MM:SS.

```
NSDateFormatter *dateFormat = [[NSDateFormatter alloc] init];
```

```
[dateFormat setDateFormat:@"HH:mm:ss"];
[dateFormat setTimeZone:[NSTimeZone timeZoneForSecondsFromGMT:0.0]];
```

Finally we want to take the NSDate and convert it into a string so that we can easily push it to our label, providing our users with a way to see our output.

```
NSString *timeString = [dateFormat stringFromDate:timeDate];
self.timeLabel.text = timeString;
```

Altogether our method should now look like this.

```
- (void)updateTimer
{
    NSDate *dateNow = [NSDate date];
    NSTimeInterval interval = [dateNow timeIntervalSinceDate:self.
startDate];
    NSDate *timeDate = [NSDate dateWithTimeIntervalSince1970:interval];

    NSDateFormatter *dateFormat = [[NSDateFormatter alloc] init];
    [dateFormat setDateFormat:@"HH:mm:ss"];
    [dateFormat setTimeZone:[NSTimeZone timeZoneForSecondsFromGMT:0.0]];

    NSString *timeString = [dateFormat stringFromDate:timeDate];
    self.timeLabel.text = timeString;
}
```

Now that we have our method set up, we need to fire it off somehow. The best way to do this is to use the NSTimer watchTimer that we set up earlier in order to trigger the method every second.

> **Note** It is important to note that if you wish to time in milliseconds, for example, the Apple Watch can sometimes struggle to process this and it is best to switch the processing over so that the iPhone handles this. The Apple Watch copes perfectly with a timer firing off every second, however any quicker than this and it starts to struggle and can provide inaccurate timings.

Inside of our IBAction for our start button that we created earlier, we want to first assign our NSDate startDate with our current time.

```
- (IBAction)startTime {
    self.startDate = [NSDate date];
}
```

Next we want to trigger our updateTimer method every second, which we do using our NSTimer.

```
- (IBAction)startTime {
        self.startDate = [NSDate date];
        self.watchTimer = [NSTimer scheduledTimerWithTimeInterval:1.0
        target:self
```

```
    selector:@selector(updateTimer)
    userInfo:nil
    repeats:YES];
}
```

Here we see that the timer is set with an interval of one second and we have set repeats to YES in order to continually fire the timer. Now that we have a fully working timer, you can now build and run the application, press START and you will get a fully working timer!

Adding the Lap Functionality

Now that we have our working stopwatch timer, the last step is to add some code to our Lap button in order to allow our application users to record their lap times.

The first step here is to add a label to our user interface, which will display our time when the Lap button is pressed. Doing this is simple. Head over to your Interface. storyboard and place a label from our object library below our Start and Lap buttons. At this stage you may want to center your label by setting its horizontal position to center in the Attributes Inspector (see Figure 2.2).

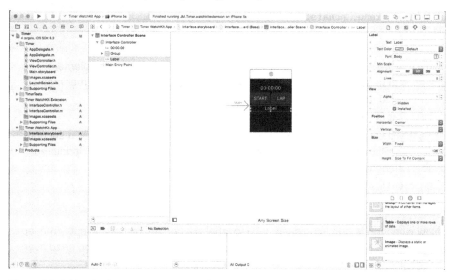

Figure 2.2. Adding lap functionality to our interface

Next we need to head over to our Assistant Editor by selecting the icon in the top right hand corner of your Xcode window. As we did in previous sections, we want to link the label on our interface to our InterfaceController.h and we do this by control clicking the label and dragging it into our .h file. Let's call it lapLabel so that it is easy to remember.

While we are in our InterfaceController.h file we want to create one more property, an NSString that will remember our time values so that they can be assigned to our label. At the bottom of our .h file, just before @end, add a new property.

```
@property (strong, nonatomic) NSString *lapTimeRecord;
```

Our InterfaceController.h file should now altogether look like this:

```
#import <WatchKit/WatchKit.h>
#import <Foundation/Foundation.h>

@interface InterfaceController : WKInterfaceController

@property (weak, nonatomic) IBOutlet WKInterfaceLabel *timeLabel;
- (IBAction)startTime;
- (IBAction)lapTime;
@property (strong, nonatomic) NSTimer *watchTimer;
@property (strong, nonatomic) NSDate *startDate;
@property (weak, nonatomic) IBOutlet WKInterfaceLabel *lapLabel;
@property (strong, nonatomic) NSString *lapTimeRecord;
@end
```

Now that we have our .h file set up, the rest of the code is easy to implement. The first step is to head over to our InterfaceController.m and in our updateTimer method we want to add the following line before our closing bracket.

```
self.lapTimeRecord = timeString;
```

This is will save the current time elapsed into the string that we created a second ago, lapTimeRecord. The last step is to head to our IBAction lapTime to update our lap label when the button is pressed.

```
- (IBAction)lapTime {
    self.lapLabel.text = self.lapTimeRecord;
}
```

Now when the button is pressed, the lap label will update itself and display the lap time. We now have a finished basic stopwatch application; make sure you head over to Xcode and test out the application!

If you want to carry on from here and improve the application you may want to consider the following:

- Storing your lap times in an array and presenting them in a table instead of a label.

- Adding a pause button to the application.

- Adding milliseconds to your time elapsed.

Timer

Arguably the most important feature of a timing device is the facility to be able to set a countdown timer. These kinds of timers become useful when you need to complete something in a specific amount of time or as a reminder to the user that something needs to be done at a specific time. A practical example is the age old one of cooking an egg. Users want to be able to set the time it takes to cook an egg and be reminded when it is finished. The Apple Watch is the perfect device to have such a timer and it is easy to implement in Xcode. The following tutorial will walk you through how to built a countdown timer application for your Apple Watch device.

Creating the User Interface

The first step is to create the user interface and lay out the various elements of the application. To do this, head over to your Interface.Storyboard within your WatchKit application. For this application we are going to have two buttons that allow the user to select the hours and minutes of their timer. We want these buttons to sit side-by-side each other so as explained in the previous Stopwatch tutorial, place a group from the object library followed by two buttons with their widths set to 0.5. To finish off the buttons change the first button's label to say 0 and the second button's to 00 to indicate our hours and minutes.

Underneath the buttons we want to place a label. Don't worry too much about setting any placeholder text because this will initially be hidden and only appear when we want it to. We'll talk more about this later on in the tutorial.

Finally we want two more buttons: named START and a RESET. As above we'll want these to sit side-by-side, so hold them within a group to accomplish this.

We now have a user interface for our application! If you've laid it out correctly, you should have something that looks like Figure 2.3.

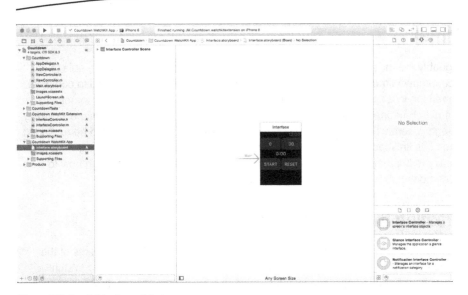

Figure 2.3. Our finished user interface

Outlets and Actions

Our next step is to hook up our interface elements into our application and set up our InterfaceController.h file. To accomplish this simply open the Assistant Editor by clicking the icon in the upper right hand corner, pressing control on each element, and dragging them into our .h file. We want to give each of our four buttons both an Outlet and an Action.

```
@property (weak, nonatomic) IBOutlet WKInterfaceButton *hourButton;
@property (weak, nonatomic) IBOutlet WKInterfaceButton *minButton;
@property (weak, nonatomic) IBOutlet WKInterfaceButton *startButton;
@property (weak, nonatomic) IBOutlet WKInterfaceButton *resetButton;

- (IBAction)hourButtonPress;
- (IBAction)minButtonPress;
- (IBAction)startButtonPress;
- (IBAction)resetButtonPress;
```

The last element that you have to hook up is the label, which will display the countdown time. We will call this timeLabel.

```
@property (weak, nonatomic) IBOutlet WKInterfaceLabel *timeLabel;
```

There are a few more things that we should do at this stage while we are in our InterfaceController.h file. The first of which is to create an NSTimer, which we will use to trigger our countdown process. To do this we simply need to add another property into our .h file.

```
@property (nonatomic, weak) NSTimer *timer;
```

Lastly, we need to create an integer that will handle how many seconds there are left remaining on our time and two NSStrings that will keep track of the hours and minutes our users have selected. We want to put these within our @interface declaration to ensure that this is made available globally across our class.

```
@interface InterfaceController : WKInterfaceController{
    int secondsRemaining;
    NSString *minValue;
    NSString *hourValue;
}
```

Altogether our InterfaceController.h file should now look something like this.

```
#import <WatchKit/WatchKit.h>
#import <Foundation/Foundation.h>

@interface InterfaceController : WKInterfaceController{
    int secondsRemaining;
    NSString *minValue;
    NSString *hourValue;
}
@property (nonatomic, weak) NSTimer *timer;

@property (weak, nonatomic) IBOutlet WKInterfaceButton *hourButton;
@property (weak, nonatomic) IBOutlet WKInterfaceButton *minButton;
@property (weak, nonatomic) IBOutlet WKInterfaceButton *startButton;
@property (weak, nonatomic) IBOutlet WKInterfaceButton *resetButton;
@property (weak, nonatomic) IBOutlet WKInterfaceLabel *timeLabel;
- (IBAction)hourButtonPress;
- (IBAction)minButtonPress;
- (IBAction)startButtonPress;
- (IBAction)resetButtonPress;

@end
```

Here we can see that we have declared each of our elements within our Apple Watch application as well as creating an NSTimer to handle our countdown and an integer to hold the time remaining, in seconds.

Initializing the Application

Now that we have a user interface and all of its elements declared, we can now focus on our InterfaceController.m file and start processing our time. Before we start processing we want to hide our label until it is necessary for it to appear. To do this you want to set the label's hidden property to YES in your awakeWithContext.

```
- (void)awakeWithContext:(id)context {
    [super awakeWithContext:context];
    _timeLabel.hidden = YES;
}
```

By setting this hidden property to YES, we are telling the Apple Watch application to hide the time label when it loads, ensuring that the user does not see the element until it is neccesary.

Handling Text Input with WatchKit

We now have to find a way to allow users to enter the time that they wish to countdown from into the application. Even though the Apple Watch itself is not meant to be an input device, with developers favoring input to be done via iPhone, there is a way we can efficiently enter data, WKTextInput. By using WKTextInput you set a series of values that users can select, for instance for our timer give our users the option to select a value of the hour to 1,2,3,4,5, and so on.

The first step in this process for our timer application is to set WKTextInput for our hour button. To do this enter the code in Listing 2.1 into your hourButtonPress IBAction.

Listing 2.1. *Setting WKTextInput for our button*

```
- (IBAction)hourButtonPress {
        NSArray* predefinedAnswer = @[@"1", @"2", @"3", @"4", @"5", @"6",
@"7",
        @"8", @"9", @"10", @"11", @"12", @"13", @"14", @"15", @"16", @"17",
@"18",
        @"19", @"20", @"21", @"22", @"23", @"24"];
        [self presentTextInputControllerWithSuggestions:predefinedAnswer
        allowedInputMode:WKTextInputModeAllowAnimatedEmoji
        completion:^(NSArray *results) {
        if (results && results.count >0) {
}
```

Here you can see that we are setting an array with all of our predefined selections in it, our hours from 1 to 24. We are then calling the WKTextInput mode with the suggestions from our array. The final part of the code tells the application that if a selection has been made the hourButton title is to be changed to that selection value and our NSString hourValue is to remember that result.

> **Note** You can set a higher number of hours for your timer, however, for the purposes of this tutorial we are choosing a maximum of 24.

We now want to repeat this process but this time for our minButtonPress IBAction (see Listing 2.2). Because this is setting our minutes, we want to create our predefined values to be our minutes from 1 to 59.

Listing 2.2. Setting our predefined values

```
- (IBAction)minButtonPress {
        NSArray* predefinedAnswer = @[@"1", @"2", @"3", @"4", @"5", @"6",
@"7",
        @"8", @"9", @"10", @"11", @"12", @"13", @"14", @"15", @"16", @"17",
@"18",
        @"19", @"20", @"21", @"22", @"23", @"24", @"25", @"26", @"27",
@"28",
        @"29", @"30", @"31", @"32", @"33", @"34", @"35", @"36", @"37",
@"38",
        @"39", @"40", @"41", @"42", @"43", @"44", @"45", @"46", @"47",
@"48",
        @"49", @"50", @"51", @"52", @"53", @"54", @"55", @"56", @"57",
@"58",
        @"59"];
        [self
}
```

The only difference, apart from our predefined values, is that you have to set the value to the minButton and minValue rather than our hour values, so make sure you change that.

That is all there is to initializing WKTextInput on the Apple Watch. You can now build and run your application and give it a test. You should be able to press either hour or minute button and it should bring up a list of options for you to select!

Start and Reset

Following on from using WKTextInput for our input buttons we now want to write our methods for both our start and reset buttons. When the start button is pressed we want to hide both of our input buttons, start our timer, and display the remaining time on screen for our users. Subsequently, we want our reset button to set our timer to 0 and reset the interface for our users.

The first step in writing our start button method is to hide our two buttons and bring up the time label. We do this by using .hidden and setting its value to YES or NO depending on whether we want to hide or show our element. Altogether our code is as follows.

```
- (IBAction)startButtonPress {
    _timeLabel.hidden = NO;
    _minButton.hidden = YES;
    _hourButton.hidden = YES;
}
```

The next step requires some calculations because we want to convert our hours and minutes set earlier into the number of seconds remaining. To calculate this we take our minute value and multiply it by 60 (the number of seconds in a minute) and our hour value by 3600 (the number of seconds in an hour.

```
secondsRemaining = ([minValue intValue] * 60) + ([hourValue intValue] *
3600);
```

The final addition to our startButtonPress method we need to make is an IF statement that triggers our timer at certain intervals. Because we want to update our time every second, we are safe to select an interval time of 1.0. We will be creating a timer method, which we will call runTimer proceeding this step so we should declare that as our selector now. It is also important to set repeats to YES to ensure that the timer continues to fire off after the button has been pressed.

```
if (secondsRemaining >0 && secondsRemaining <36000001 ) {
        _timer = [NSTimer scheduledTimerWithTimeInterval:1.0 target:self
selector:@selector(runTimer:) userInfo:nil repeats:YES];
    }
```

We now can create our reset button. The code for this is considerably simpler than that of our start button because all we need to do is show/hide the appropriate elements of our user interface and invalidate our timer object using the following.

```
[_timer invalidate];
```

Now that we have created both of our methods for our buttons the resulting code should look like this.

```
- (IBAction)startButtonPress {
    _timeLabel.hidden = NO;
    _minButton.hidden = YES;
    _hourButton.hidden = YES;
    secondsRemaining = ([minValue intValue] * 60) + ([hourValue intValue] *
3600);
    if (secondsRemaining >0 && secondsRemaining <36000001 ) {
        _timer = [NSTimer scheduledTimerWithTimeInterval:1.0 target:self
selector:@selector(runTimer:) userInfo:nil repeats:YES];
    }
}

- (IBAction)resetButtonPress {
    _minButton.hidden = NO;
    _hourButton.hidden = NO;
    _timeLabel.hidden = YES;
    [_timer invalidate];
}
```

Creating our Timer Method

Carrying forward what we have already created, now comes the all important timer method. This particular method is what counts down our time, updates our label, and issues an action whenever the timer reaches 0. The first thing that we have to do is create the method in our InterfaceController.m file. You should call it something that you will remember because we'll have to relate to it further on in the tutorial. For this example we will call it runTimer.

```
- (void)runTimer: (NSTimer *) runningTimer {}
```

Now that we have our method, we want to create two integers, hoursValue, and minutesValue, which will store our hours and minutes figures respectively so that they can be displayed on screen.

```
- (void)runTimer: (NSTimer *) runningTimer {
int hoursValue, minutesValue;
}
```

The next step is to countdown our timer by one each time the method is fired. To do this we use the "--" operator on our secondsRemaining value we created earlier.

```
- (void)runTimer: (NSTimer *) runningTimer {
    int hoursValue, minutesValue;
    secondsRemaining--;
}
```

Now we wish to update our time label every time this method fires, thus creating the countdown effect visually for our users. To perform this action we first have to calculate our hours and minutes value from the second we have. First we calculate the hours value by dividing the seconds remaining by 3600, we then set this to our hoursValue integer we created a second ago. Then work out how many minutes by using the integer remaining operator, which in Objective-C we write as "%". Finally we set our label to display the correct time remaining using NSString stringWithFormat. Altogether we should now have a method that looks like this.

```
- (void)runTimer: (NSTimer *) runningTimer {
    int hoursValue, minutesValue;
    secondsRemaining--;
    hoursValue = secondsRemaining / 3600;
    minutesValue = (secondsRemaining % 3600) / 60;
    _timeLabel.text =[NSString stringWithFormat:@"%02d:%02d", hoursValue,
minutesValue];
}
```

Every time this method runs it will deduct a second from our time and update the display in our app accordingly.

The final part of this method is to perform some sort of action whenever the time reaches 0. To accomplish this we simply use an IF statement to detect whether or not the time has reached 0 and if this is true then it performs some kind of action. We must be sure to invalidate the timer when the countdown reaches 0 to ensure that our users can use the application as many times as they want. The result of our IF statement is as follows.

```
if (secondsRemaining==0) {
        [_timer invalidate];
        //PERFORM YOUR ACTION HERE
    }
```

You can perform any kind of function when the timer reaches 0, you may want to play an alert sound for instance, have an on-screen notification, or have the Watch vibrate at the necessary time.

Believe it or not, our entire timer application is now complete! You can now head over to Xcode and test it out. If you are looking to work on this project further you may want to consider the following areas of improvement:

- Adding seconds to the timer

- Enabling dictation for user input

- Using force touch to tap the user on the wrist when the timer reaches 0

Calendar

When the Apple Watch was brought to the forefront, a handful of applications were announced that would be natively available on the device from day one. With time very much the focus of a lot of people's attentions, it wasn't a far stretch to imagine how useful a calendar application might be on the Apple Watch. In this section we will look at how various elements of a calendar application are constructed including how to effectively use iCloud and EventKit. We will also explore how to create a calendar application from scratch, detailing the process of building a user interface and saving an event to your iCloud calendar before exploring the different types of notification available within WatchKit at your disposal.

Introduction to iCloud

When Apple first introduced the iCloud API alongside Cloudkit in 2014, it meant that developers could unlock a lot of potential in their devices. For the first time there was now one reliable, unified way of sharing information between devices and storing information in a reliable and cohesive way. In this section we will go over the basics of iCloud including how to configure your project for iCloud, and creating record types.. Outlined below are some of the many features of iCloud that help developers reach their full potential within their applications.

- Notifications

- 1 PB Asset Storage (Images, Audio, etc.)

- 10 TB Database Storage (Strings, Arrays, etc.)

Setting up your Xcode Project for iCloud

The first step that you have to do within your Xcode project is to enable iCloud for use. To do this head over to the capabilities section and flick on the switch from OFF to ON, this is enable iCloud. At this stage you will have to select your developer account from the drop-down list. Once this is done, press OK. Within the iCloud settings, underneath where it says Services, tick the box next to CloudKit to enable CloudKit for your project (see Figure 2.4).

Figure 2.4. iCloud Capabilities settings

Creating Record Types

Now that we have set up CloudKit we now want to create Records for the various elements that we want to use within our application. You can think of records as shelves in a library, they hold the data that you are going to store and are named in accordance to the containing information.

Initially we want to click on the CloudKit Dashboard button, which will take us to the iCloud webpage. At this stage you'll be promoted to sign in using your Apple Developer username and password. You will be presented with a page that looks like Figure 2.5.

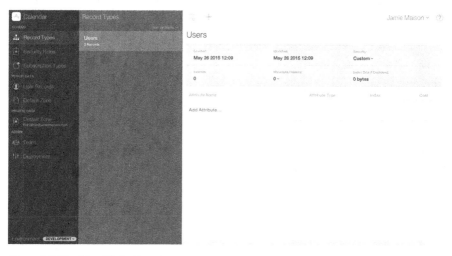

Figure 2.5. The CloudKit dashboard

To create a new record type for CloudKit you must first select Record Types from the left-hand menu, you may notice that you will already have a record named Users, which you can ignore. We want to click the "+" icon to create a new record (see Figure 2.6).

Figure 2.6. Adding a new record

The next step is to enter your Record Type Name, think of this as your shelf in your library, so you'll want to keep your data types in mind and name it accordingly. Proceeding on from this you now want to add in your various attributes or data types. You can select from the drop-down menu next to the attribute what kind of data you'd like to assign. You can assign the following types of attribute:

- String

- Date/Time

- Integer

- Double

- Bytes

- Location

- Reference

- Asset

A good example of a record would be a book (see Figure 2.7). Your record type name would be Book and the attributes may be things like a string for title, a string for author, an integer for pages, and a date/time for publish date. This is just an example, however it gives you a good idea of the kinds of data you can store using CloudKit.

Figure 2.7. Record example – Book

Now that we know the basics of iCloud and CloudKit we can use it to create our calendar application using iCloud together with EventKit.

Creating Calendars and Events in iOS Using EventKit and iCloud

Apple's EventKit framework provides "classes for accessing and manipulating calendar events and reminders." When it was introduced, it allowed developers an easy way to create and manage calendar applications, in a way that was easy than previously possible. In this section we will look at EventKit and learn the basics, including using EventKit with iCloud, with a view to using it later on in this chapter to create a calendar application for the Apple Watch.

Creating a New Calendar

The first step that is vital when using EventKit is to enable the framework within your Xcode project. To do this you simply need to head over to the General tab of your Xcode target and click the "+" symbol under Linked Frameworks And Libraries. Following on from that all you need to do is select EventKit.framework from the list and click Add, you have now successfully added EventKit to your project. Whenever you use EventKit you will also have to remember to add it to the headers of your project by adding the following into your .h files.

```
#import <EventKit/EventKit.h>
```

Creating a new calendar using EventKit is far simpler than you would think. The idea is that all you have to do is tell Xcode that you want to create a calendar, and then indicate both the calendar title and the source. To do this you first need to create the calendar within your onLoad or awakeWithContext method.

```
EKEventStore *eventStore = [[EKEventStore alloc] init];
EKCalendar *calendar = [EKCalendar calendarWithEventStore:eventStore];
calendar.title = @"myCalendar";
```

Here you can see that we create a calendar and set its title to myCalendar. The next step is to set the calendar source, which we do by looping through the existing source types within the Event Store until we find the one we want, then all we have to do is tell our calendar to use that source.

```
EKSource *calSource = nil;
for (EKSource *source in eventStore.sources) {
    if (source.sourceType == EKSourceTypeLocal) {
        calSource = source;
        break;
    }
```

```
    }
        if (calSource) {
            calendar.source = calSource;
        }
    }
```

This code shows that you can set the calendar to be stored locally only on the user's device, but what if we want to create a calendar within iCloud? In this instance all we have to replace is the sourceType we are looking for in our loop to iCloud, which results in the following code.

> **Note** You can only set a local calendar if iCloud is NOT ENABLED within your application.

```
EKSource *calSource = nil;
    for (EKSource *source in eventStore.sources) {
        if (source.sourceType == EKSourceTypeCalDAV && [source.title
isEqualToString:@"iCloud"]) {
            calSource = source;
            break;
        }
    }
        if (calSource) {
            calendar.source = calSource;
        }
    }
```

Here you can see that we have replaced the sourceType from local to iCloud. This will mean that your calendar is saved on iCloud and accessibile across any iOS or OSX device.

Creating an Event

Now that we have learned how to create a calendar using the EventKit framework, we can turn our attention to creating the events that exist within them. The first step is to create an EKEvent by writing the following code.

```
    EKEvent *newEvent = [EKEvent eventWithEventStore:eventStore];
```

Following on from this you then want to set both your start and end dates of your event.

```
NSDate *startDate = [NSDate date];
    newEvent.startDate = startDate;
    newEvent.endDate = [startDate dateByAddingTimeInterval:3600];
```

Here you can see that we've set the start date to the current date and the end date to an hour after our start date. Obviously you can set the start and end date in accordance with whatever event you are creating. After doing this you need to tell you new event that it is part of the eventStore you wish to save to.

```
[newEvent setCalendar:[eventStore defaultCalendarForNewEvents]];
```

The final step when creating in an event is saving it to our calendar, which we do by simply using saveEvent as follows.

```
[eventStore saveEvent:newEvent span:EKSpanThisEvent error:&err];
```

With this code we are telling our application to save our event to our calendar that we created. That is all that there is to creating a calendar with EventKit and iCloud, and creating an event. In the next section we will look at how we can use this to create a functioning calendar application for Apple Watch that allows the user to receive push notifications on their device.

Creating an Apple Watch Calendar Application

In this section we are going to utilize what we have learned in the previous sections and create a calendar application for the Apple Watch. By the end of this tutorial you will have learned everything there is to know about creating a basic calendar application with the Apple Watch in mind. We will be using iCloud and EventKit in order to create the application while exploring push notifications on the Apple Watch itself.

Enabling iCloud and EventKit

The very first step that we should take after creating our Xcode project and WatchKit extension is to enable iCloud and EventKit for use within our application. The process is identical to the previous chapters, however we will re-cap what needs to be done.

iCloud

- Enable iCloud in the Capabilities section of your target.

- Select your developer account from the drop-down list.

- Enable CloudKit by ticking the box in the Services section.

EventKit

- Click the "+" button underneath the Linked Frameworks and Libraries segment under the General tab of your target.

- Select the EventKit.framework from the list and click "Add".

- Remember to add #import <EventKit/EventKit.h> in every .h file you wish to include EventKit in.

> **Note** Remember to initiate both iCloud and EventKit for both your iPhone application and WatchKit Extension target if you have decided to do your processing on the iPhone.

UI

Carrying on forward from our iCloud and EventKit initialization, we now want to set up our user interface for our application. At this point it may be useful to understand how this application will work. As it may be favorable to do the majority of the processing on our iPhone companion application because it will be far more powerful, we are going to set up an iPhone application that allows our users to enter a start time and end time of their event, and then give them the option to save this event to their Calendar. The Apple Watch application will then allow the users to receive a notification when their event is triggered.

It is with this in mind that we can head over to our Main.Storyboard within our iPhone application and start positioning our elements. The first objects that we should place in from our Object Library are our two text fields. It may be useful to add placeholder text to either field in order to make using the application easier. This can be done by clicking the relevant object and navigating to the Attributes Inspector. From there you can enter the placeholder text in the section marked Placeholder, something like Start Time and End Time may be appropriate for our two text fields.

The final element in our user interface is a button that will save our event when clicked. As before, drag this element over into your storyboard and you can give it a title of Save, or something similar.

Now that we have added our elements into our storyboard we should have something that looks similar to Figure 2.8.

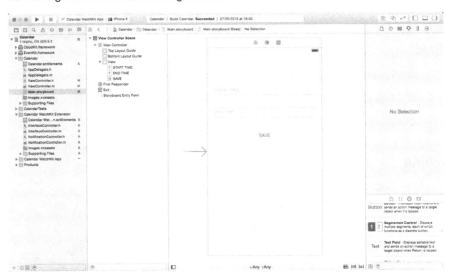

Figure 2.8. Finished user interface

The final step in producing our user interface is to navigate over to our ViewController.h and defining our elements. As in previous sections, all we have to do here is open the Assistant Editor by clicking the icon in the top right hand corner of Xcode and keeping our storyboard and .h files side-by-side. Then all you have to do is control click the elements and drag them over to your header file to include them. We want to create two IBOutlets for our text fields, named something like startField and endField. We also want to create an IBAction linked to our save button, which we can call saveButton or similar. Our entire header file will now be laid out as follows.

```
#import <UIKit/UIKit.h>
#import <EventKit/EventKit.h>
@interface ViewController : UIViewController
@property (weak, nonatomic) IBOutlet UITextField *startField;
@property (weak, nonatomic) IBOutlet UITextField *endField;
- (IBAction)saveButton:(id)sender;
@end
```

Create Calendar

Since we have now set up the elements of our user interface we can move over to the main code to be executed within our calendar application. The first component that we should set up is creating a global variable for our eventStore, which we do by including the following in our interface declaration.

```
@interface ViewController (){
    EKEventStore *eventStore;
}
```

This simply creates an EKEventStore for us to use throughout our application.

After this we need to initialize our calendar and store it in iCloud. Because we want this to happen immediately after starting our application, we want to write the following within our viewDidLoad.

```
eventStore = [[EKEventStore alloc] init];
EKCalendar *calendar = [EKCalendar calendarWithEventStore:eventStore];
calendar.title = @"iCloudCalendar";

EKSource *calSource = nil;
for (EKSource *source in eventStore.sources) {
    if (source.sourceType == EKSourceTypeCalDAV && [source.title
isEqualToString:@"iCloud"]) {
        calSource = source;
        break;
    }
}
if (calSource) {
    calendar.source = calSource;
}
```

When executed, this code creates a calendar with a title of iCloudCalendar (You can name it whatever you wish) and assigns it the source type of iCloud; thus indicating that it is an iCloud calendar. Believe it or not, that is all we have to do when initializing our calendar for the first time!

Saving Our Event

Arguably one of the most important aspects of your calendar application will be the facility to create and save events reliably. With this in mind we can now begin working on our all-important save button which, when pressed, will take the dates entered into our startField and endField and create an event in reference to those dates.

The first part of our button's code will be to convert the string entered into our field into an NSDate. This is necessary in order for EventKit to process our dates entered so that it can turn them into our event. To perform this task we want to use NSDateFormatter, which will convert our string into a date. The code will look like this.

```
NSDateFormatter *dateFormat = [[NSDateFormatter alloc] init];
[dateFormat setDateFormat:@"dd-MM-yyyyz"];
NSDate *startDate = [dateFormat dateFromString:_startField.text];
```

Here we can see that NSDateFormatter is taking the string from our startField text field and converting it to an NSDate in the format dd-MM-yyyy. You may notice the lowercase "z" at the end of the setDateFormat. All this does is ensure that the date you have entered is in a non-location format ensuring that the time doesn't compensate for time zones GMT, BST, etc. Be sure to repeat this code for both the startField and endField text fields so that both are formatted correctly for further use.

The next part of our core relates to actually creating the event using EventKit and saving it to our calendar. To do this we simply create a new event using EKEvent, set our dates, and save the event to our calendar. This results in the following code.

```
EKEvent *newEvent = [EKEvent eventWithEventStore:eventStore];

newEvent.startDate = startDate;
newEvent.endDate = endDate;

[newEvent setCalendar:[eventStore defaultCalendarForNewEvents]];

NSError *err;

[eventStore saveEvent:newEvent span:EKSpanThisEvent error:&err];
```

If we look at this segment closer, we see that we are initially creating an EKEvent called "newEvent" which we then reference to when setting our start and end dates. We then set our newEvent to the eventStore that we created earlier. We will be using the NSError in our code in the next part of our tutorial, however it is necessary to define it here so it can be referenced to in our saveEvent. The last line of code here simply tells our eventStore to save our new event to our iCloud calendar.

The last step is to use the NSError that we just created in order to create some alerts that notify the user whether or not the event has saved. This is as simple as using an if statement to determine if there is an error and showing a UIAlertView depending on the result. You should end up with something that looks like what is shown in Listing 2.3.

Listing 2.3. Creating alerts for saved events

```
if (err == noErr) {
        UIAlertView *alert = [[UIAlertView alloc]
                                initWithTitle:@"New Event"
                                message:[NSString
stringWithFormat:@"Successfully added to calendar!"]
                                delegate:nil
                                cancelButtonTitle:@"OK"
                                otherButtonTitles:nil];
        [alert show];
    }
    else{
        UIAlertView *errorAlert = [[UIAlertView alloc]
                                initWithTitle:@"Error Creating Event"
                                message:[NSString stringWithFormat:@"There
has been an error creating your event"]
                                delegate:nil
                                cancelButtonTitle:@"OK"
                                otherButtonTitles:nil];
        [errorAlert show];

    }
```

Now that we have set up the save button to handle our event, saving our InterfaceController.m will be as shown in Listing 2.4.

Listing 2.4. Our new InterfaceController.m

```
#import "ViewController.h"

@interface ViewController (){

    EKEventStore *eventStore;
}

@end

@implementation ViewController

- (void)viewDidLoad {
    [super viewDidLoad];

    eventStore = [[EKEventStore alloc] init];
    EKCalendar *calendar = [EKCalendar calendarWithEventStore:eventStore];
    calendar.title = @"iCloudCalendar";

    EKSource *calSource = nil;
    for (EKSource *source in eventStore.sources) {
        if (source.sourceType == EKSourceTypeCalDAV && [source.title
isEqualToString:@"iCloud"]) {
            calSource = source;
            break;
        }
    }
```

```
    if (calSource) {
        calendar.source = calSource;
    }
}

- (IBAction)saveButton:(id)sender {

    NSDateFormatter *dateFormat = [[NSDateFormatter alloc] init];
    [dateFormat setDateFormat:@"dd-MM-yyyyz"];
    NSDate *startDate = [dateFormat dateFromString:_startField.text];

    NSDateFormatter *dateFormat2 = [[NSDateFormatter alloc] init];
    [dateFormat setDateFormat:@"dd-MM-yyyyz"];
    NSDate *endDate = [dateFormat2 dateFromString:_endField.text];

    EKEvent *newEvent = [EKEvent eventWithEventStore:eventStore];

    newEvent.startDate = startDate;
    newEvent.endDate = endDate;

    [newEvent setCalendar:[eventStore defaultCalendarForNewEvents]];

    NSError *err;

    [eventStore saveEvent:newEvent span:EKSpanThisEvent error:&err];

    if (err == noErr) {
        UIAlertView *alert = [[UIAlertView alloc]
                                initWithTitle:@"New Event"
                                message:[NSString
stringWithFormat:@"Successfully added to calendar!"]
                                delegate:nil
                                cancelButtonTitle:@"OK"
                                otherButtonTitles:nil];
        [alert show];
    }
    else {
        UIAlertView *errorAlert = [[UIAlertView alloc]
                                initWithTitle:@"Error Creating Event"
                                message:[NSString stringWithFormat:@"There
has been an error creating your event"]
                                delegate:nil
                                cancelButtonTitle:@"OK"
                                otherButtonTitles:nil];
        [errorAlert show];
    }
}
@end
```

Now that we have set up the iPhone side of our calendar application, we can talk about notifications on the Apple Watch and we can explore potential ways of how you would go about delivering notifications for your calendar application.

Notifications on the Apple Watch

When Apple announced the Apple Watch it became evident that the predominant feature of the device would be in its user notifications, acting as a convenient and easy to reach the notification center for iOS. With this in mind developers are always interested to know about how notifications work on the Apple Watch. In this section we will cover the different types of notification you can get on the Apple Watch, which you may want to use in relation to your calendar application.

There are two types of notification in WatchKit, short-look and long-look. Each type has its particular nuances, which are as follows:

- Short-look notifications work in exactly the same way as notifications work on the iPhone. As a developer we do not have any control over the way that short-look notifications are laid out and are therefore the easiest way of delivering a notification on the Apple Watch. The way that they work is that the short-look notification will appear on whichever is the active device, the Apple Watch or the iPhone. They appear just like a banner notification does on the iPhone.

- Long-look notifications by nature can be categorized as either a static or dynamic notification.

- Static notifications have a single text field that is automatically filled by the system. You can customize the title of the notification and the sash color, but are otherwise entirely static.

- Dynamic notifications, on the contrary, can have their own custom interface, which can be created using your Interface. storyboard.

Now that you understand the different types of notification you can have on the Apple Watch, you can explore which one suits your application the best. Typically a short-look notification is powerful when you want to quickly push a notification to the user. A static long-look notification is useful when wanting to hold the users attention a little longer and a dynamic notification allows you to adapt their experience.

Summary

Throughout the course of this chapter we have examined some of the apps that run seamlessly on the Apple Watch and are fundamentally the type of applications that will be successful on the platform. We have looked at the stopwatch together with the art of timing accurately with WatchKit. We have built a basic timer application while discussing text input on the Apple Watch. Finally we examined some of the basic functions of the calendar, exploring upon iCloud, and how to save an event with

EventKit. Hopefully you now have a good knowledge of some of the fundamentals behind these types of WatchKit applications and that you can now explore these features further and build yourself a functional and successful application on watchOS.

Chapter 3

Taming Complex Data for the Watch

By Matt Klosterman, creator of various Watch apps

Five seconds.

One. Two. Three. Four. Five.

Those five seconds are roughly the amount of time you have in your Watch application to grab the attention of the user and fulfill the expectations they had when they raised their wrist and opened your application.

It may seem like a daunting challenge. When creating a Watch experience for an application that connects to any large data source, it is very likely that just describing the types of information available to your users would take far, far longer than five seconds.

What is a developer to do? How can you give a user the information or action they need within such a short span of time?

This chapter will walk you through four techniques that were successful in taking one such large system, an application for an airline, and turning it into a delightful experience that could truly tell you what you needed to know in five quick seconds. As the chapter progresses we'll walk through a more general example of a complicated application, a CRM system, and work through exercises that show you how to apply these four techniques for creating simple and useful Watch applications for complex information. These techniques are:

1.   Find your user's story.

2.   Maintain simplicity through relevancy.

3.   Increase recognition through repetition.

4.   Use notifications as punctuation.

Background

Before we tackle each of these techniques, let's decide on the application we are building. This application is going to be a CRM (Customer Relationship Management) system that is aimed at commercial photographers. These are the types of professional photographers whose specialty is taking photographs for usage in things like advertising campaigns.

Five to 10 years ago, software that assisted this photographer may have ran on a desktop computer. It may have looked something like Figure 3.1.

Figure 3.1. Wireframe of CRM software for photography niche on Mac

As iPhones and iPads became more prevalent over the last five years, that software may have started to look more like Figure 3.2.

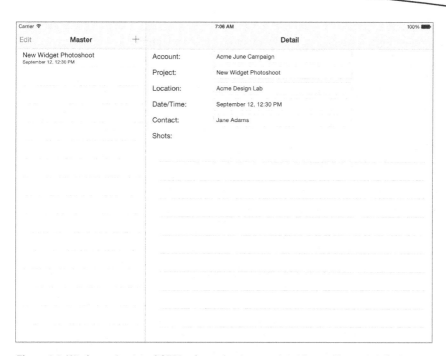

Figure 3.2. Wireframe drawing of CRM software for photography niche on iPhone and iPad

What would that same information look like if you were trying to bring it to a Watch? If we tried to directly translate what we had on the desktop and then on a phone or tablet onto the Watch, we wouldn't have a very useful application (see Figure 3.3).

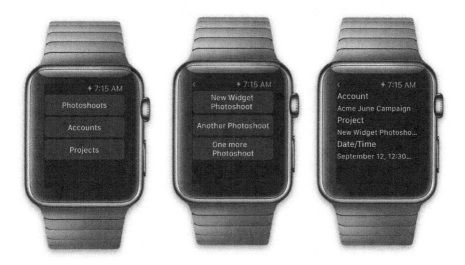

Figure 3.3. Wireframe of native implementation of CRM software for photography niche on Watch

One thing that should be clear is that simply taking an existing UI that successfully navigates through a complex hierarchy of information and "shrinking it down" to fit on the screen of the Watch is not going to be ideal. Two key factors contribute to this. First, only small snippets of information are visible at a time. Second, holding both of your hands up and navigating through different tiers of information would quickly become awkward.

There must be a better way. In fact there is, and we are going to start walking through one approach that does work better right now. To do so we're going to think like an assistant. For this particular application that we are building, a CRM application for commercial photographers, we are going to pretend we are the assistant to a photographer.

As their assistant, the photographer relies on you for information, instructions and the handling of tasks. You provide them support in keeping their clients happy and ensure their photo shoots happen on schedule and to the desired specifications.

How would you do this job if you were a piece of software? More precisely, how would you do this job if every interaction you had with your boss was limited to, say, five to twenty seconds? Could you get their attention within five seconds? Could you keep their job flowing smoothly if there was a hard cap of twenty seconds each time you talked? That's the reality of what your users are going to expect when using your Watch application. Interactions longer than that can quickly make the user feel awkward or frustrated. So how do we proceed?

Find Your User's Story

Our first goal is going to be to find the user's story. What matters to them? What problems are they having? What information or actions will we provide to solve those problems?

Let's continue by putting ourselves in the shoes of the assistant again. The photographer you work for may be very busy. Between shoots they may ask you questions about what they need to do. Questions like:

- When is the next shoot?
- Where is it at?
- Who is it for?
- What is it of?

What other questions could we anticipate? Let's generalize the questions a bit further to:

- Who?
- What?
- When?

- Where?

- Why?

- How?

In journalism, those six questions represent what must be answered to tell a complete story. In this hypothetical job as an assistant, this is also a great place to start for figuring out what information to focus on presenting to your employer. If the photographer whom you work for rushes by you in the office and says, "get me up to speed" what would you say? You might say something like:

"In one hour, we need to leave to go across town to Acme's design laboratory to take some shots of their new widget for next month's ad campaign."

How would we take complexity out of some one else's life? What questions would we answer for them? That's the heart of what we need to solve to successfully take a system of complex data and distill it down into simple answers for the person. This is the essential starting place for creating a successful Watch application.

For an application that is assisting a commercial photographer, the core answers at a single point in time might look something like Figure 3.4.

Figure 3.4. Simple UI that answers the questions of where, when, what, and who

With this display we've answered the core questions that the photographer might ask while running by us inside their office:

- Where is the next shoot?

- When is it?

- What is it of?

- Who is it for?

Now that we've narrowed in on the questions we need to answer, let's start creating a simple project to display this information.

CREATE A SIMPLE APPLICATION TO DISPLAY 'WHAT'S NEXT'

1. Start a new project in Xcode by choosing File ➤ New ➤ Project.

2. We are going to focus on the Watch side of the application so let's just create a simple Single View Application. If you are using Xcode 7 and building for watchOS 2 you'll choose watchOS ➤ Application ➤ iOS App with WatchKit App (see Figure 3.5).

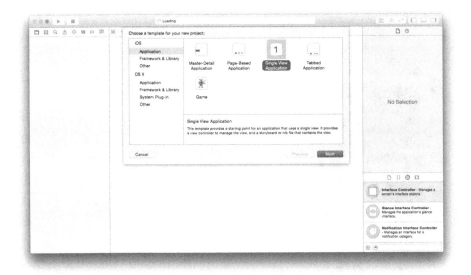

Figure 3.5. Creating a single view app

3. We'll call this project Chapter6 (see Figure 3.6). If you are using Xcode 7 and building for watchOS 2 you'll choose to include a Notification Scene and a Complication, but not a Glance Scene right now.

Figure 3.6. Naming our project Chapter6

4.   Navigate to where you wish to save the project and choose Create (see Figure 3.7).

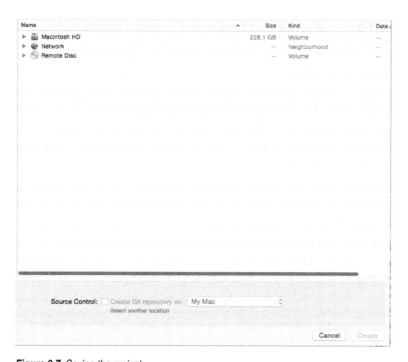

Figure 3.7. Saving the project

5.   Next we'll add a Watch target to the application. If you are using Xcode 7 and building for watchOS 2   you'll skip steps 5 through 10.

6.   To add the Watch target, we will next choose the project at the top level of the Project Navigator in Xcode (see Figure 3.8).

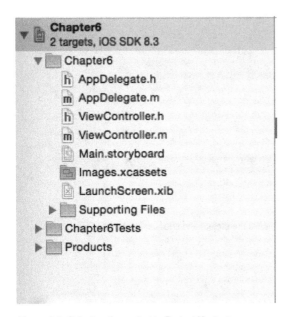

Figure 3.8. Selecting the project in Project Navigator

7.   At the bottom left of the left hand pane in the project editor, we'll press the "+" button to create a new Target (Figure 3.9).

Figure 3.9. Selecting our target

8.   We will choose to create a WatchKit App target, and then press Next (Figure 3.10).

Figure 3.10. Creating our WatchKit app

9.   For now, we will choose to create both a Notification scene but not a Glance scene, and then we will press Finish (see Figure 3.11).

Choose options for your new target:

Product Name:	Chapter6 WatchKit App
Organization Name:	Example
Organization Identifier:	com.example.Chapter6
Bundle Identifier:	com.example.Chapter6.watchkitapp
Language:	Objective-C
	☑ Include Notification Scene
	☐ Include Glance Scene
Project:	📄 Chapter6
Embed in Application:	🅰 Chapter6

Cancel   Previous   Finish

Figure 3.11. Creating a Notification scene

10.   When prompted we will choose to activate the Chapter 6 WatchKit App Scheme (Figure 3.12).

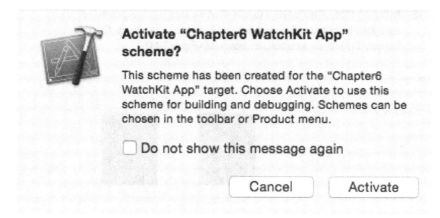

Activate "Chapter6 WatchKit App" scheme?

This scheme has been created for the "Chapter6 WatchKit App" target. Choose Activate to use this scheme for building and debugging. Schemes can be chosen in the toolbar or Product menu.

☐ Do not show this message again

Cancel   Activate

Figure 3.12. Activating the scheme

11. Next, we'll navigate to the Interface.storyboard file for the Watch application.

12. Xcode created a Main interface for our Watch application as well as a placeholder for our first notification (see Figure 3.13).

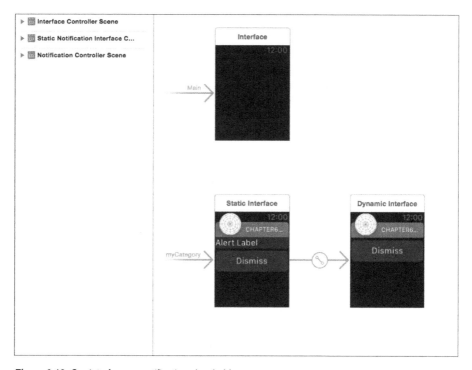

Figure 3.13. Our interface an notification placeholder

13. Before we chose to not create a Glance when we were having Xcode set up our initial WatchKit app. If we had there would also be a placeholder Glance Interface Controller in Interface.storyboard (see Figure 3.14).

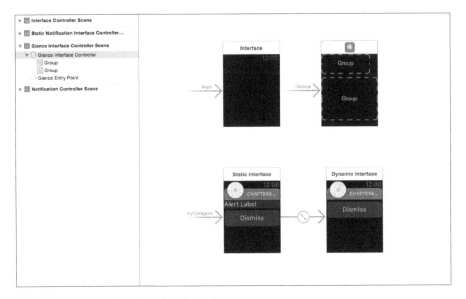

Figure 3.14. Note the Glance Interface Controller

14. To start with on our sample application, we are actually going to start by focusing on the Glance. To make demonstrating some of the later exercises easier we are actually going to create the Glance in a separate storyboard.

15. Right-click Chapter6 WatchKit App in the project navigator, and click New File (Figure 3.15).

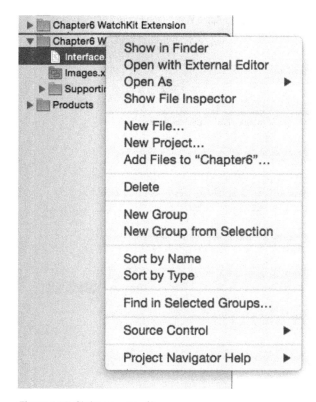

Figure 3.15. Clicking our new file

16.   We are going to choose Storyboard under Apple Watch (see Figure 3.16).

Figure 3.16. Selecting Storyboard

17. We are going to call this Storyboard Glance1. When you create multiple
    Storyboards and include them all in an Apple WatchKit application they become
    joined together in the final WatchKit application that is installed on the Watch.
    This is an important distinction because each application can only have one
    Glance interface specified in the application (Figure 3.17).

Figure 3.17. Naming the Storyboard Glance1

18.   After creating the Storyboard we will have a new, empty storyboard (Figure 3.18).

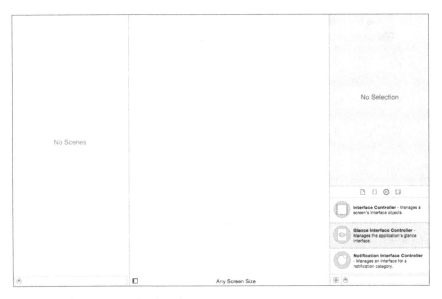

Figure 3.18. *Our new empty Storyboard*

19.   We are going to create a new Glance by dragging a Glance Interface Controller onto the Storyboard (Figure 3.19).

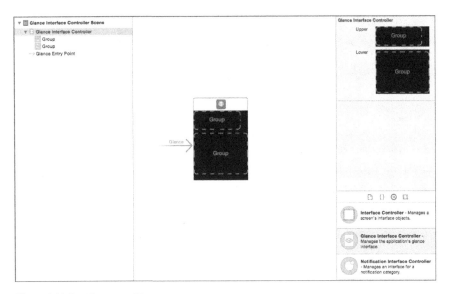

Figure 3.19. *Creating a new Glance*

20. For this example we are going to stay with the default Glance template of a group in the top section, and a group in the bottom section.

21. As a reminder, here is the UI we are aiming to create right now (Figure 3.20).

Figure 3.20. *Our UI we are creating*

22. To model this we are going to start by changing the Layout of the bottom Group from Horizontal to Vertical (Figure 3.21).

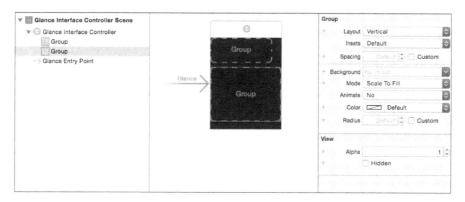

Figure 3.21.*Changing to vertical*

23.   Next we are going to put four WKInterfaceLabels into that bottom group (Figure 3.22).

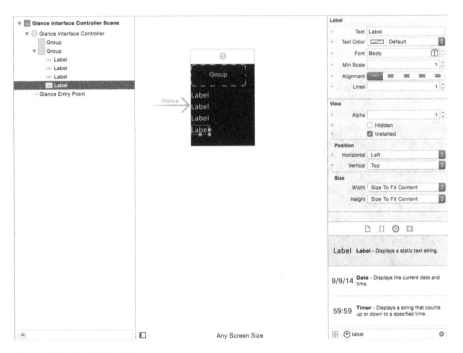

Figure 3.22. Adding four labels

24.   For now, we will hard code the text in these labels (Figure 3.23).

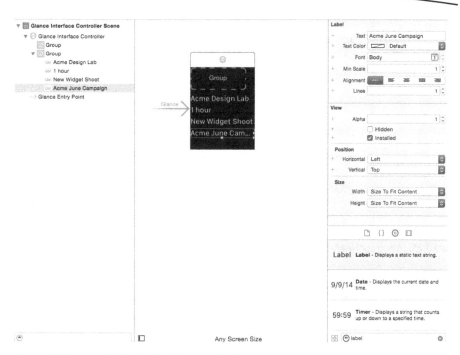

*Figure 3.23.*Temporarily hardcoding text on our labels

25. Right away we notice one issue. Some of our text may be too large to fit the width of the display. To handle this we are going to change the labels to allow text to shrink instead of clip if the text runs outside of the bounds of the labels. For now, we'll set the Min Scale on each label to .5 (Figure 3.24).

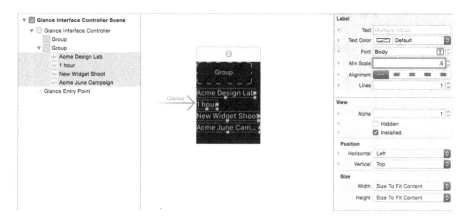

Figure 3.24. Setting our Min Scale to .5

26. With those settings we are still a little off from what our design called for though.

The design called for a different font weight on the When? line, the 1 hour value. To achieve that we are going to set the font style on that label to Headline (Figure 3.25).

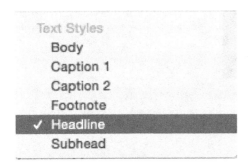

Figure 3.25. *Setting our Headline font style*

27. When we set a font to one of those preset Text Styles, it allows the user's Dynamic Type preferences in settings to change the size and weight of the default system font settings to match the user's preference for text sizes (Figure 3.26).

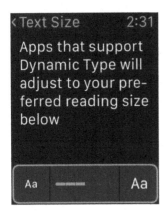

Figure 3.26. *Dynamic text in action*

28. To further emphasize that line of text we are going to set the other lines to use

style Caption 2.

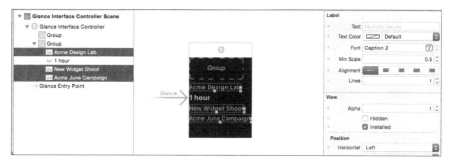

Figure 3.27. Setting font style to caption 2

29. Let's run our application to get a sense of what our UI looks like as of right now.

30. To run our Glance we'll want to pick it from the scheme list in Xcode.

31. At this point we'll see a problem (see Figure 3.28).

Figure 3.28.We are missing our Glance scheme

32. Since we created our Glance by hand and didn't have one when we created the project, Xcode didn't automatically create a scheme for our Glance. We'll create that now.

33. First we'll choose Manage Schemes.

34. Next we'll highlight our Chapter6 WatchKit App scheme (Figure 3.29).

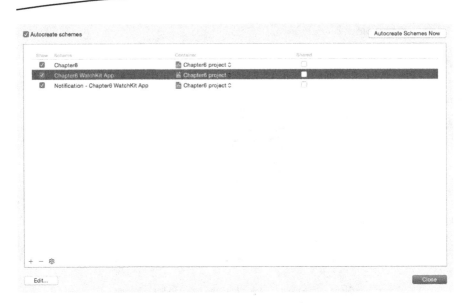

Figure 3.29. Highlighting our scheme

35. Next we'll choose the gear icon near the bottom left of the window and click it. We will then choose to Duplicate the highlighted scheme (see Figure 3.30).

Figure 3.30. Duplicating a scheme

36. After choosing Duplicate we will be prompted to edit settings for the new Scheme (Figure 3.31).

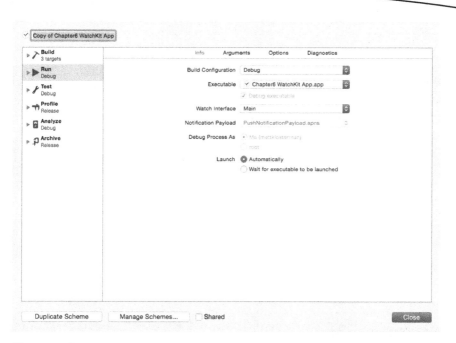

Figure 3.31. Edit the scheme settings

37.   We will name our scheme Chapter6 WatchKit App - Glance and we will set the Watch Interface setting to Glance. Then we'll press Close (Figure 3.32).

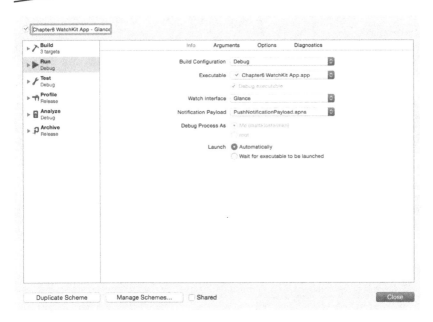

Figure 3.32. Setting the interface to Glance

38.   Then we'll press Close on the schemes Window as well.

39.   Now we'll run the application with our new Chapter6 Watch App - Glance scheme.

40.   We now have our simple UI running as a Glance (Figure 3.33).

Figure 3.33. Our running Glance

Maintain Simplicity Through Relevancy

We've now created a simple application that displays a small sliver of data to our user that answers their most immediate questions:

- When is the next shoot?

- Where is it at?

- Who is it for?

- What is it of?

The information we have to provide to the user could still be far more involved than that. Let's revisit again what the CRM software for this niche may have looked like as a Mac application a number of years ago (see Figure 3.34).

Figure 3.34. Wireframe of CRM software for photography niche on Mac

Is there a way we can make more of this information available to the user in a Watch application? If we do attempt to display more information to the user, how can we do so without making the software so complex that it takes minutes instead of seconds to help the user?

To answer these questions, let's think about those questions the photographer may ask a bit more. What questions might the photographer ask if they were on location at a shoot instead of in their studio? The questions on location might be more along the lines of:

- When does this shoot need to be completed by?

- Who is my point of contact for the client?

- Why is the client doing the shoot?

- What shots do I need to get?

For this scenario we may instead want our application to display the answers to those questions. It may look something like what is shown in Figure 3.35.

Figure 3.35. Simple UI that answers the questions of why, when, who, and what for a photographer that is on location at a shoot

With this modified layout of information for when the user is on location we now have an interface that can still convey the most important thing the photographer needs to know at that moment of time. It is also simple, clear and concise so that the photographer can digest it in just a few seconds.

Let's look at the interfaces for these two scenarios side-by-side (see Figure 3.36).

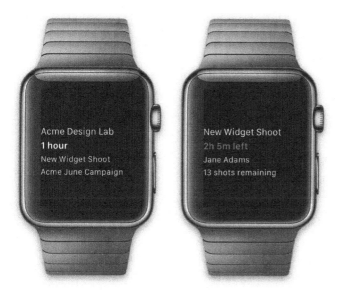

Figure 3.36. Basic UI for two scenarios side-by-side

What we've accomplished with this design is to maintain the simplicity of the user interface by varying the content that is displayed instead of expanding the amount of content that is displayed. By focusing on displaying the most relevant information we can maintain a user interface that is easily understood within seconds. What is important right now is surfaces in front of the user. Everything else falls out of sight.

How would we go about implementing such a design? With our next exercise we'll start by modifying our application to support both types of scenarios: in studio and on location.

MODIFY APPLICATION TO SUPPORT 'ON-LOCATION' SCENARIO

1.   Open our Chapter 6 Project in Xcode.

2.   We're going to start by just creating a different hard coded Glance again for demonstration purposes. To do this we will create a duplicate of our Glance storyboard. Note that steps 3 through 16 aren't actually required for the project to function, and are instead a short detour to give a bit of insight into the fact that WatchKit storyboard files get combined together at compile time before being put into the application bundle that resides on the Watch.

3.   In Xcode, right-click on Glance1.storyboard and choose Show in Finder (Figure 3.37).

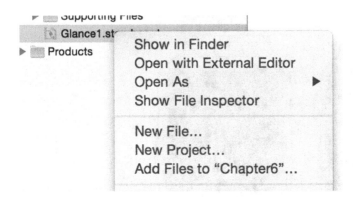

Figure 3.37. Selecting Show in Finder

4.   In Finder, right-click Glance1.storyboard and click Duplicate In Finder. Right-click Glance1.storyboard and click Duplicate (see Figure 3.38).

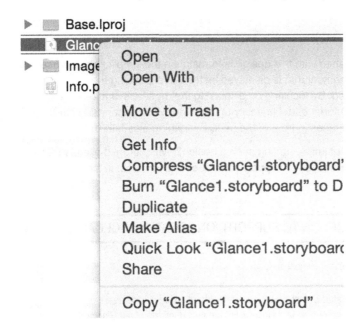

Figure 3.38. Choosing the duplicate

5.   You will now have the Glance1.storyboard and Glance1 copy.storyboard files (Figure 3.39).

Figure 3.39. Both Glance1 copies

6.   Rename Glance1 copy.storyboard to Glance2.storyboard (Figure 3.40).

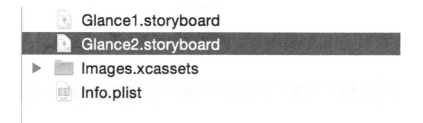

Figure 3.40. Renaming the Glances

7.   Drag Glance2.storyboard into your Xcode project below Glance1.storyboard.
     When prompted add it to the Chapter6 WatchKit App target. Leave Copy Items
     If Needed selected and click Finish. Drag Glance2.storyboard into your Xcode
     project below Glance1.storyboard. When prompted add it to the Chapter6
     WatchKit App target, and leave Copy Items If Needed selected, and click Finish
     (see Figure 3.41).

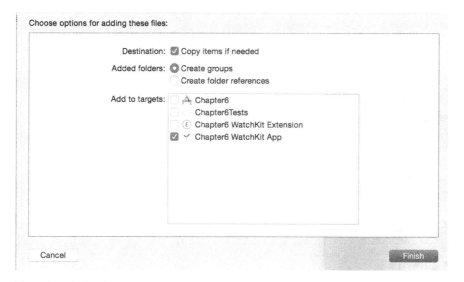

Figure 3.41. Adding Glances to the WatchKit App

8. If we ran the application now with both storyboard files in the project we would get an error about the application having two Glances defined. For this demonstration we'll leave Glance2.storyboard enabled in the Chapter6 WatchKit App target (Figure 3.42).

Figure 3.42. Keeping Glance2 enabled

9. We will disable the Glance1.storyboard in the Chapter6 WatchKit App target (Figure 3.43).

Figure 3.43. Disabling Glance1

10. If we were to re-run our application now, we'd get the same UI as before (Figure 3.44).

Figure 3.44. The same UI

11. But we want to visually inspect our alternate design for the application when the
     user is on-location at a photo shoot (Figure 3.45).

Figure 3.45. Visual inspection

12. To do this we are simply going to edit the labels to have the new text, and then
     we are going to set the color on the time label to be red (Figure 3.46).

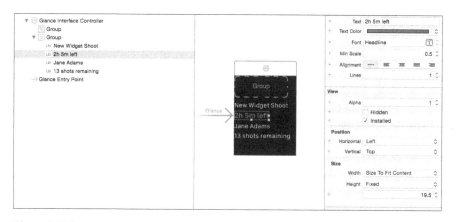

Figure 3.46. Setting our time label to red

13.   When we run the application we will now see the alternate UI (Figure 3.47).

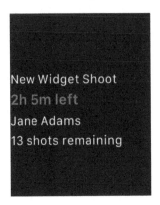

Figure 3.47. Our alternate UI

14.   Two hard coded UIs aren't particularly useful, so let's clean up our project and work on setting up the application to switch between scenarios programmatically.

15.   First delete the Glance2.storyboard file.

16.   Next select the Glance1.storyboard file in the project navigator.

17.   Next select our Glance Interface Controller in Interface Builder (Figure 3.48).

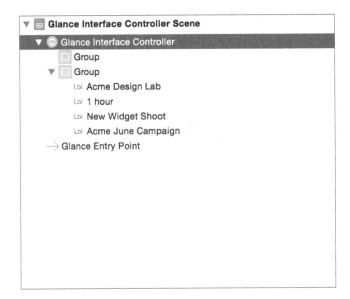

Figure 3.48. Selecting the Glance Interface Controller

18. Copy that controller by choosing Edit, and then Copy.

19. Now select our main Interface.storyboard file for our Watch application.

20. Click in an empty location in the Storyboard in Interface Builder.

21. Then paste in our Glance using Edit, and then Paste. We'll now have four interface controllers in our Storyboard. A main interface, a Glance, and a static and dynamic notification interface controller for the myCategory notification category (see Figure 3.49).

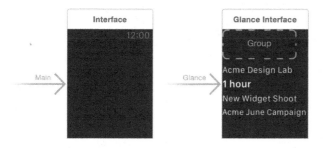

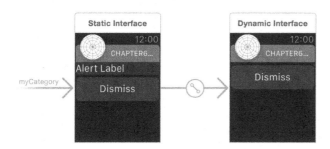

Figure 3.49. Our four interface controllers

22. Next, we'll clean up our project by deleting the Glance1.storyboard file.

23. Now we'll start on building out the code for our sample application. First, we'll right-click the Chapter6 WatchKit Extension group in the project navigation and choose New File (Figure 3.50).

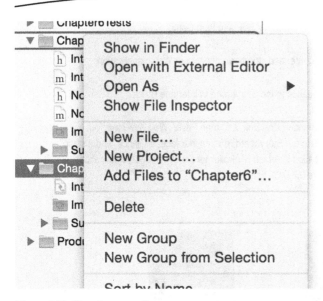

Figure 3.50. *Choosing a new file*

24. We'll choose to create a new iOS Cocoa Touch Class and then click Next (Figure 3.51).

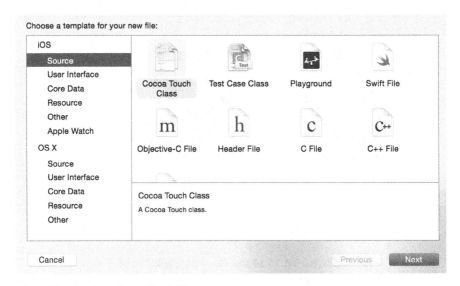

Figure 3.51. *Creating a Cocoa Touch Class*

25. We are going to name our new class GlanceController, and make it a Subclass of WKInterfaceController. Then we will click Next (Figure 3.52).

Choose options for your new file:

Class:	GlanceController
Subclass of:	WKInterfaceController
	Also create XIB file
	iPhone
Language:	Objective-C

Cancel   Previous   Next

Figure 3.52. Our new class and subclass

26.   We'll double check that our new class is added to the WatchKit Extension, and
       then we'll click Create (Figure 3.53).

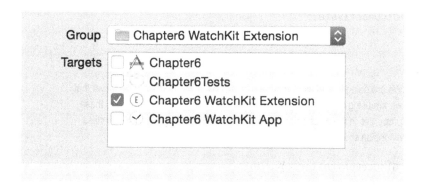

Group   Chapter6 WatchKit Extension

Targets   ☐ Chapter6
             ☐ Chapter6Tests
             ☑ ⓔ Chapter6 WatchKit Extension
             ☐ Chapter6 WatchKit App

Figure 3.53. Adding our new class to the WatchKit extension

Xcode will create a new class that looks similar to this:

```
//
//  GlanceController.m
//  Chapter6

#import "GlanceController.h"
```

```
@interface GlanceController ()

@end

@implementation GlanceController

- (void)awakeWithContext:(id)context {
    [super awakeWithContext:context];

    // Configure interface objects here.
}

- (void)willActivate {
    // This method is called when watch view controller is about to be
visible to user
    [super willActivate];
}

- (void)didDeactivate {
    // This method is called when watch view controller is no longer
visible
    [super didDeactivate];
}

@end
```

27. We are going to add four properties to match the WKInterfaceLabel views that
     we are using to display our summary information to the user. We'll add these
     properties in the class extension at the top of GlanceController.m. The class
     extension should now look like this:

```
@interface GlanceController ()

@property (nonatomic,weak) IBOutlet WKInterfaceLabel *userSummaryLine1;
@property (nonatomic,weak) IBOutlet WKInterfaceLabel *userSummaryLine2;
@property (nonatomic,weak) IBOutlet WKInterfaceLabel *userSummaryLine3;
@property (nonatomic,weak) IBOutlet WKInterfaceLabel *userSummaryLine4;

@end
```

28. Now we will go back to our Interface.storyboard and do two things. First, we'll
     click on our Glance and set the class to GlanceController in the identity inspector
     (Figure 3.54).

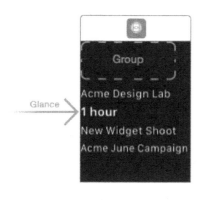
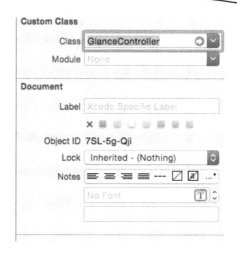

Figure 3.54. Setting the class to GlanceController

29. Next we will connect our labels in the storyboard to the outlets of the properties we added to the Glance's class extension (Figure 3.55).

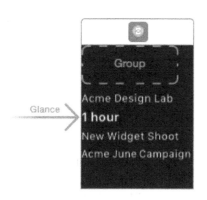
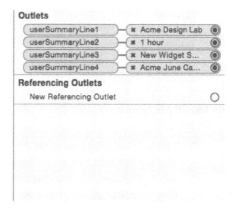

Figure 3.55. Connecting our labels

30. Now we are going to create some sample data and set up our GlanceController to support two different summary views of our user's data. One for while the user is on location at a shoot, and one for when the user is not on location at a shoot.

31. We're going to add four new classes to the project plus add a plist that we'll use as our data store for demonstration purposes. We'll also need to add the CoreLocation framework to the linked libraries and frameworks for our WatchKit Extension's target.

32. We'll add our sample data plist file first. Right-click the Chapter6 WatchKit Extension group, and click New File.

33. Choose Property List in the iOS Resource section.

34. Click Next.

35. Name the file SampleData and click Create.

36. The contents of the plist should look like Figure 3.56.

Key		Type	Value
▼ Root	○	Dictionary	(1 item)
▼ photoshoots		Array	(1 item)
▼ Item 0		Dictionary	(9 items)
locationBeacon		String	799723ED-3AA3-4FA8-B745-B7EE371F94B1
locationName		String	Acme Design Lab
▼ locationCoordinate		Dictionary	(2 items)
latitude		Number	38.059666
longitude		Number	-97.954506
beginTime		String	2015-09-12T17:30:00Z
endTime		String	2015-09-12T21:30:00Z
shootDescription	○ ○	String	○ New Widget Shoot
projectDescription		String	Acme June Campaign
clientContactName		String	Jane Adams
▼ plannedShots		Array	(3 items)
▼ Item 0		Dictionary	(2 items)
shotDescription		String	Shot 1
completed		Boolean	NO
▼ Item 1		Dictionary	(2 items)
shotDescription		String	Shot 2
completed		Boolean	YES
▼ Item 2		Dictionary	(2 items)
shotDescription		String	Shot 3
completed		Boolean	NO

Figure 3.56 The plist contents

37. Next we'll create four new classes. For each class add a new file to the WatchKit Extension and choose Cocoa Touch Class. All of them are going to subclass NSObject. The four class names are Photoshoot, ShotInformation, PhotoshootManager, and PhotoshootSummarizer. The code for each is as follows.

```
//
//  Photoshoot.h
//  Chapter6

#import <Foundation/Foundation.h>
#import <CoreLocation/CoreLocation.h>

@interface Photoshoot : NSObject

@property (nonatomic,strong) NSString *locationName;
```

```objc
@property (nonatomic,assign) CLLocationCoordinate2D locationCoordinate;
@property (nonatomic,strong) NSUUID *locationBeacon;

@property (nonatomic,strong) NSDate *beginTime;
@property (nonatomic,strong) NSDate *endTime;

@property (nonatomic,strong) NSString *shootDescription;
@property (nonatomic,strong) NSString *projectDescription;

@property (nonatomic,strong) NSString *clientContactName;

@property (nonatomic,strong) NSArray *plannedShots;

- (instancetype)initWithDictionary:(NSDictionary *)dictionary NS_
DESIGNATED_INITIALIZER;

@end

//
//  Photoshoot.m
//  Chapter6

#import "Photoshoot.h"
#import "ShotInformation.h"

@implementation Photoshoot

- (instancetype)initWithDictionary:(NSDictionary *)data
{
    self = [super init];

    if (!self) {
        return nil;
    }

    self.locationName = data[@"locationName"];
    self.locationCoordinate = CLLocationCoordinate2DMake([data[@"locati
onCoordinate"] [@"latitude"] doubleValue], [data[@"locationCoordinate"]
[@"longitude"] doubleValue]);
    self.locationBeacon = [[NSUUID alloc] initWithUUIDString:data[@"lo
cationBeacon"]];
```

```
    self.beginTime = [self dateForRFC3339DateTimeString:data[@"beginTi
me"]] ?: [NSDate distantPast];
    self.endTime = [self dateForRFC3339DateTimeString:data[@"endTime"]]
?: [NSDate distantPast];
    self.shootDescription = data[@"shootDescription"];
    self.projectDescription = data[@"projectDescription"];
    self.clientContactName = data[@"clientContactName"];


    NSMutableArray *plannedShots = [NSMutableArray array];


    [data[@"plannedShots"] enumerateObjectsUsingBlock:^(NSDictionary
*shotData, NSUInteger idx, BOOL *stop) {
        ShotInformation *shot = [[ShotInformation alloc]
initWithDictionary:shotData];
        [plannedShots addObject:shot];
    }];


    self.plannedShots = plannedShots;


    return self;
}


// Modified example code from https://developer.apple.com/library/ios/
qa/qa1480/_index.html
- (NSDate *)dateForRFC3339DateTimeString:(NSString *)
rfc3339DateTimeString
// Returns a user-visible date time string that corresponds to the
// specified RFC 3339 date time string. Note that this does not handle
// all possible RFC 3339 date time strings, just one of the most common
// styles.
{
    static NSDateFormatter *    sRFC3339DateFormatter;
    NSString *                  userVisibleDateTimeString;
    NSDate *                    date;

    // If the date formatters aren't already set up, do that now and
cache them
    // for subsequence reuse.

    if (sRFC3339DateFormatter == nil) {
```

```
        NSLocale *                      enUSPOSIXLocale;

        sRFC3339DateFormatter = [[NSDateFormatter alloc] init];

        enUSPOSIXLocale = [NSLocale localeWithLocaleIdentifier:@"en_US_
POSIX"];

        [sRFC3339DateFormatter setLocale:enUSPOSIXLocale];
        [sRFC3339DateFormatter setDateFormat:@"yyyy'-'MM'-
'dd'T'HH':'mm':'ss'Z'"];
        [sRFC3339DateFormatter setTimeZone:[NSTimeZone
timeZoneForSecondsFromGMT:0]];
    }

    // Convert the RFC 3339 date time string to an NSDate.
    // Then convert the NSDate to a user-visible date string.

    userVisibleDateTimeString = nil;

    date = [sRFC3339DateFormatter dateFromString:rfc3339DateTimeStri
ng];

    return date;
}

@end

//
//  ShotInformation.h
//  Chapter6

#import <Foundation/Foundation.h>

@interface ShotInformation : NSObject

@property (nonatomic,strong) NSString *shotDescription;
@property (nonatomic,assign,getter=hasBeenCompleted) BOOL completed;

- (instancetype)initWithDictionary:(NSDictionary *)shotData NS_
DESIGNATED_INITIALIZER;
```

```objc
@end
//
//  ShotInformation.m
//  Chapter6


#import "ShotInformation.h"


@implementation ShotInformation

- (instancetype)initWithDictionary:(NSDictionary *)shotData
{
    self = [super init];

    if (!self) {
        return nil;
    }

    self.shotDescription = shotData[@"shotDescription"];
    self.completed = [shotData[@"completed"] boolValue];

    return self;
}

@end

//
//  PhotoshootManager.h
//  Chapter6
//


#import <Foundation/Foundation.h>

@interface PhotoshootManager : NSObject

+ (NSArray *)photoshoots;

@end

//
//  PhotoshootManager.m
//  Chapter6
```

```objc
//

#import "PhotoshootManager.h"
#import "Photoshoot.h"

@implementation PhotoshootManager

+ (NSArray *)photoshoots
{
    // In a real application we would utilize Core Data or another data
storage approach.
    // In that case we may write out the shared data to an App Group
container directory
    // so that both the WatchKit extension and our main app can access
the data directly.
    NSString *sampleDataPath = [[[NSBundle mainBundle] resourcePath] st
ringByAppendingPathComponent:@"SampleData.plist"];
    NSDictionary *sampleData = [NSDictionary dictionaryWithContentsOfFi
le:sampleDataPath];

    NSArray *shootDictionaries = sampleData[@"photoshoots"];

    NSMutableArray *photoShoots = [NSMutableArray array];

    [shootDictionaries enumerateObjectsUsingBlock:^(NSDictionary
*shootDictionary, NSUInteger idx, BOOL *stop) {
        Photoshoot *shoot = [[Photoshoot alloc] initWithDictionary:sho
otDictionary];

        [photoShoots addObject:shoot];
    }];

    return photoShoots;
}

@end

//
// PhotoshootSummarizer.h
// Chapter6
//
```

```objc
#import <Foundation/Foundation.h>

@interface PhotoshootSummarizer : NSObject

+ (NSDictionary *)currentSummaryInformation:(NSArray *)photoshoots;

@end

//
//  PhotoshootSummarizer.m
//  Chapter6
//

#import "PhotoshootSummarizer.h"

#import "Photoshoot.h"
#import "ShotInformation.h"

@implementation PhotoshootSummarizer

+ (NSDictionary *)currentSummaryInformation:(NSArray *)photoshoots
{
    Photoshoot *mostRelevantShoot = [self
mostRelevantShoot:photoshoots];

    // If there isn't a relevant shoot we'll return an information
summary
    if (mostRelevantShoot) {
        if (arc4random() % 2 == 0) {
            return [self summaryInformationForOnLocationShoot:mostRele
vantShoot];
        } else {
            return [self summaryInformationForShoot:mostRelevantShoot];
        }
    }
    return [self summaryInformationForNoRelevantShoot];
}

+ (Photoshoot *)mostRelevantShoot:(NSArray *)shoots
{
    // Initial rule: the most relevant shoot is the soonest to occur.
```

```objc
    // Future rules could be added e.g. a shoot that is nearby is more
    // relevant than one schedule to happen soon
    return [shoots firstObject];
}


+ (NSDictionary *)summaryInformationForNoRelevantShoot
{
    return @{
             @"line1" : @"No photoshoots scheduled",
             };
}


+ (NSDictionary *)summaryInformationForOnLocationShoot:(Photoshoot *)
shoot
{
    __block NSInteger completedShots = 0;
    [shoot.plannedShots enumerateObjectsUsingBlock:^(ShotInformation
*shot, NSUInteger idx, BOOL *stop) {
        if ([shot hasBeenCompleted]) {
            completedShots++;
        }
    }];

    NSInteger remainingShots = [shoot.plannedShots count] -
completedShots;

    return @{
             @"line1" : shoot.locationName,
             @"line2" : @"#countdown#",
             @"line3" : shoot.clientContactName,
             @"line4" : [NSString stringWithFormat:@"%td shots
remaining", remainingShots],
             @"relevantStart" : shoot.beginTime,
             @"relevantEnd" : shoot.endTime,
             };
}


+ (NSDictionary *)summaryInformationForShoot:(Photoshoot *)shoot
{
    return @{
             @"line1" : shoot.locationName,
```

```
            @"line2" : @"#countdown#",
            @"line3" : shoot.shootDescription,
            @"line4" : shoot.projectDescription,
            @"relevantStart" : shoot.beginTime,
            @"relevantEnd" : shoot.endTime,
            };
}

@end
```

38. Each of these classes has a purpose. Photoshoot and ShotInformation model the data in our sample data. PhotoshootManager provides a way for us to get our sample data out of our data store. The most important for this exercise is PhotoshootSummarizer. Its job is to apply business rules to distill down all of our data that we may have in our data store into a simple four line summary for the user at any point in time.

39. To utilize PhotoshootSummarizer we are going to modify the code in GlanceController. GlanceController.m should now look like this:

```
//
//  GlanceController.m
//  Chapter6

#import "GlanceController.h"

#import "Photoshoot.h"

#import "PhotoshootSummarizer.h"
#import "PhotoshootManager.h"

@interface GlanceController ()

@property (nonatomic,weak) IBOutlet WKInterfaceLabel *userSummaryLine1;
@property (nonatomic,weak) IBOutlet WKInterfaceLabel *userSummaryLine2;
@property (nonatomic,weak) IBOutlet WKInterfaceLabel *userSummaryLine3;
@property (nonatomic,weak) IBOutlet WKInterfaceLabel *userSummaryLine4;

@property (nonatomic,strong) NSDictionary *userSummaryInformation;

@end
```

```objc
@implementation GlanceController

- (void)awakeWithContext:(id)context {
    [super awakeWithContext:context];

    [self.userSummaryLine1 setText:@""];
    [self.userSummaryLine2 setText:@""];
    [self.userSummaryLine3 setText:@""];
    [self.userSummaryLine4 setText:@""];
}


- (void)willActivate {
    // This method is called when watch view controller is about to be
visible to the user
    [super willActivate];

    [self refreshData];
}

- (void)refreshData
{
    NSDictionary *userSummary = [PhotoshootSummarizer currentSummaryInf
ormation:[PhotoshootManager photoshoots]];

    NSDictionary *lastSummaryInformation = self.userSummaryInformation;

    if (![lastSummaryInformation[@"line1"] isEqualToString:userSummary
[@"line1"]]) {
        [self.userSummaryLine1 setText:userSummary[@"line1"]];
    }
    if (![lastSummaryInformation[@"line2"] isEqualToString:userSummary
[@"line2"]]) {
        [self.userSummaryLine2 setText:userSummary[@"line2"]];
    }
    if (![lastSummaryInformation[@"line3"] isEqualToString:userSummary
[@"line3"]]) {
        [self.userSummaryLine3 setText:userSummary[@"line3"]];
    }
    if (![lastSummaryInformation[@"line4"] isEqualToString:userSummary
[@"line4"]]) {
        [self.userSummaryLine4 setText:userSummary[@"line4"]];
```

```
    }

    self.userSummaryInformation = userSummary;
}

@end
```

40. What we've done in this exercise is create a glance that will show the user a simple four-line summary of their data.

Right now our application supports both in-studio and on-location scenarios, but they are just displayed at random. How can we make our application switch between them? What signals are available to our application to allow it to determine relevancy? There could be many. Some examples may be:

- User's location

- Date/time of specific photo shoots

- Unread messages from clients

- Unread messages from vendors

For our example we are going to keep it simple and just determine which scenario is relevant using the user's location. With the next two exercises we'll expand our application to switch the content displayed based on two different location signals: GPS coordinates and proximity to one or more iBeacons.

MODIFY APPLICATION TO AUTOMATICALLY SWITCH SCENARIOS USING GPS

1. Add the following to the end of –[GlanceController awakeWithContext:].

```
[self registerForNotifications];
```

2. Add the following methods to GlanceController.

```
- (void)registerForNotifications
{
    [[NSNotificationCenter defaultCenter] addObserver:self selector:@
selector(handleSummaryChange:) name:@"PhotoshootSummaryChanged"
object:nil];
}

- (void)unregisterForNotifications
{
```

```objc
    [[NSNotificationCenter defaultCenter] removeObserver:self];
}

- (void)dealloc
{
    [self unregisterForNotifications];
}

- (void)handleSummaryChange:(NSNotification *)notification
{
    dispatch_async(dispatch_get_main_queue(), ^{
        [self refreshData];
    });
}
```

      3.   Add a new class, PhotoshootLocationManager with the following code.

```objc
//
//  PhotoshootLocationManager.h
//  Chapter6
//

#import <Foundation/Foundation.h>
#import <CoreLocation/CoreLocation.h>

@interface PhotoshootLocationManager : NSObject

+ (instancetype)sharedManager;

@property (nonatomic,strong) CLLocation *lastLocation;

@end

//
//  PhotoshootLocationManager.m
//  Chapter6
//

#import "PhotoshootLocationManager.h"

@interface PhotoshootLocationManager () <CLLocationManagerDelegate>
```

```objc
@property (nonatomic,strong) CLLocationManager *manager;

@end

@implementation PhotoshootLocationManager

+ (instancetype)sharedManager {
    static dispatch_once_t pred;
    static PhotoshootLocationManager *shared = nil;
    dispatch_once(&pred, ^{
        shared = [[[self class] alloc] init];

        shared->_manager = [[CLLocationManager alloc] init];
        [shared->_manager setDelegate:shared];
        [shared->_manager startUpdatingLocation];
    });
    return shared;
}

- (void)locationManager:(CLLocationManager *)manager
didUpdateLocations:(NSArray *)locations
{
    self.lastLocation = [locations lastObject];
}

- (void)setLastLocation:(CLLocation *)lastLocation
{
    BOOL changed = !(_lastLocation.coordinate.latitude == lastLocation.
coordinate.latitude &&
                    _lastLocation.coordinate.longitude ==
lastLocation.coordinate.longitude);

    _lastLocation = lastLocation;

    if (changed) {
        [[NSNotificationCenter defaultCenter] postNotificationName
:@"PhootshootLocationChange" object:nil userInfo:@{@"newLocation":
lastLocation}];
    }
}

@end
```

4.   Add the following import to PhotoshootSummarizer.h.

```
#import "PhotoshootLocationManager.h"
```

5.   Add the following methods to PhotoshootSummarizer.m.

```objc
+ (instancetype)sharedManager {
    static dispatch_once_t pred;
    static PhotoshootSummarizer *shared = nil;
    dispatch_once(&pred, ^{
        shared = [[[self class] alloc] init];
        [shared registerForNotifications];
    });
    return shared;
}

- (void)registerForNotifications
{
    [[NSNotificationCenter defaultCenter] addObserver:self selector:@
selector(handleLocationUpdate:) name:@"PhootshootLocationChange"
object:nil];
}

- (void)unregisterForNotifications
{
    [[NSNotificationCenter defaultCenter] removeObserver:self];
}

- (void)dealloc
{
    [self unregisterForNotifications];
}

- (void)handleLocationUpdate:(NSNotification *)notification
{
    [[NSNotificationCenter defaultCenter] postNotificationName:@"Photos
hootSummaryChanged" object:nil];
}
```

6.   In PhotoshootSummarizer.m change the following.

```
if (arc4random() % 2 == 0) {
```

to

```
CLLocation *currentUserLocation = [[PhotoshootLocationManager
sharedManager] lastLocation];


    CLCircularRegion *testRegion = [[CLCircularRegion alloc] initW
ithCenter:currentUserLocation.coordinate radius:5000 identifier:@"Curr
entUserRegion"];


    if ([testRegion containsCoordinate:mostRelevantShoot.
locationCoordinate]) {
```

7.   Add the following to the beginning of + [PhotoshootSummarizer currentSummaryInformation].

```
// Behind the scenes we'll instantiate an instance of
PhotoshootSummarizer that monitors data that can affect summaries
    [self sharedManager];
```

8.   Add NSLocationAlwaysUsageDescription and NSLocationWhenInUseDescription keys to the Info.plist files of the iOS application and the WatchKit Extension.

9.   Update the iOS application to call –[CLLocationManager requestAlwaysAuthorization] at an appropriate time to allow the application and the WatchKit Extension to receive location updates while the applications are both in the foreground and background.

10.   The above changes will set up our Glance to react to the user's location to customize the view of information displayed for a particular photo shoot. We change our summary generator class (PhotoshootSummarizer) to test for a region of 5km around the user to see if the photoshoot location is in the region. If the photo shoot is located in that region, we display the on-site view of the information to the user. Our location manager class posts notifications when the user's location changes. Our summarizer class listens for types of data changing that can affect the summary (location in this state) and then posts a notification to allow consumers of summary information to get update information to display to the user.

11.   To test this out we'll run the application again. We should see what is shown in Figure 3.57.

Figure 3.57. *Our app in action*

12. Now we'll tell the Simulator that we are located near the first photo shoot in our sample data by going to the Debug menu highlighting Location, and choosing Custom. When we do that we'll enter these values for the custom location (Figure 3.58).

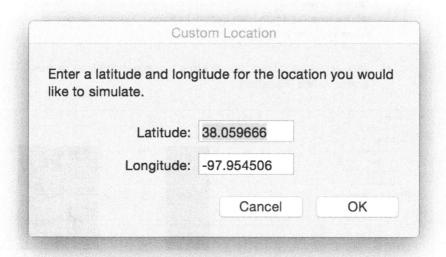

Figure 3.58. *Entering a custom location*

13. After entering these values, our Watch interface will change to the on-site view (Figure 3.59).

Figure 3.59. The new on-site view

14. There are two things we still need to do in this example. First, we are still using a placeholder token in the summary data to represent a countdown to an event happening. We need to recognize that token in our user interface and replace it with the correct user facing data. Second, for the on-site view our design calls for the countdown text being in a red color instead of white.

15. To accomplish the first item, we'll add a timer in a group along with our previous Summary 2 label (Figure 3.60).

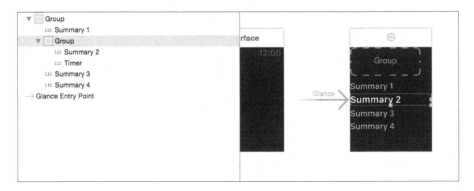

Figure 3.60. Adding a timer

16. Then we'll adjust our code to hook up this timer to data when appropriate, as well as meet the goal of changing the text color.

17. We'll create a new property to represent the timer interface object on GlanceController.

```
@property (nonatomic,weak) IBOutlet WKInterfaceTimer
*userSummaryLine2Timer;
```

18. Then we'll change the code that updates line 2 in GlanceController to be as follows.

```
if (![lastSummaryInformation[@"line2"] isEqualToString:userSummary
[@"line2"]] ||
        ![lastSummaryInformation[@"relevantStart"] isEqualToDate:userSu
mmary[@"relevantStart"]] ||
        ![lastSummaryInformation[@"relevantEnd"] isEqualToDate:userSumm
ary[@"relevantEnd"]] ||
        [lastSummaryInformation[@"onLocation"] boolValue] !=
[userSummary[@"onLocation"] boolValue]) {
        if ([userSummary[@"line2"] isEqualToString:@"#countdown#"]) {
            [self.userSummaryLine2 setHidden:YES];
            [self.userSummaryLine2Timer setHidden:NO];

            if ([userSummary[@"onLocation"] boolValue]) {
                NSDate *relevantDate = userSummary[@"relevantStart"];
                [self.userSummaryLine2Timer setDate:relevantDate];

                [self.userSummaryLine2Timer setTextColor:[UIColor
redColor]];
            } else {
                NSDate *relevantDate = userSummary[@"relevantEnd"];
                [self.userSummaryLine2Timer setDate:relevantDate];

                [self.userSummaryLine2Timer setTextColor:[UIColor
whiteColor]];
            }
            [self.userSummaryLine2Timer start];
        } else {
            [self.userSummaryLine2 setHidden:NO];
            [self.userSummaryLine2Timer setHidden:YES];
            [self.userSummaryLine2Timer stop];
```

```
                [self.userSummaryLine2 setText:userSummary[@"line2"]];
        }
}
```

19. Finally, in PhotoSummarizer.m we'll modify summaryInformationForOnLocationShoot and summaryInformationForShoot to contain an additional key/value pair. The value for on location shoots will be @ YES and @NO for other shoots.

```
        @"onLocation" : @YES,
```

20. With these changes we now have an application that will switch between the two designs we have for our user's data depending on whether the user is on location or not. From here we could extend the application to customize the information further based on many other factors. The most relevant shoot that is returned by the summarizer class could vary based on location, time, and many other factors. Within the logic to displaying the most relevant shoot, we can have the same factors impacting what the user sees just like in this example.

Increase Recognition Through Repetition

With the photographer's CRM application that we've built through our exercises so far, we've focused on building out just the Glance of our Watch application. This isn't by accident. The constrained nature of Glances has helped us hone in on what our user's story is at that moment of time in their life. With that figured out we've been able to create an interface that answers the single most likely question the user will have at a given moment in time. If we've done a good job at finding our user's story and maintaining simplicity through relevancy, we should now have an application that grabs the user's attention within those short five seconds.

What if our user has more than just five seconds? Put yourself back in the shoes of an assistant to our photographer again. This time the photographer rushes up to you and again says, "Get me up to speed." This time though instead of looking like they are ready to run across the room, they take a deep breath and pause while waiting for your response. This time you might still say:

"In one hour, we need to leave to go across town to Acme's design laboratory to take some shots of their new widget for next month's ad campaign."

But then you too may pause for a moment and add:

"Tomorrow we are doing a shoot at the beach for WidgetCo. Then on Thursday you have a consultation with WidgetMax to plan the theme for their Spring ads."

If we were to take the work we've done to build a Glance so far and use it as the basis for a Watch application UI that represents these answers for our user, it might look something like Figure 3.61.

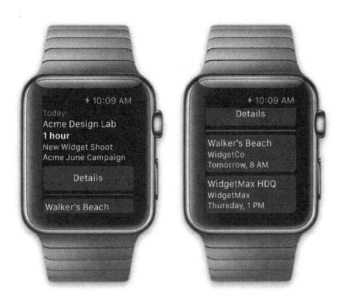

Figure 3.61. *Example UI for full Watch application that displays additional details for the user. The user can scroll down to see additional information*

What have we done here? In Figure 3.62, let's take a look at this side-by-side with our Glance from before.

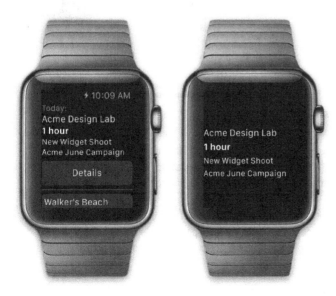

Figure 3.62. *Before and after view of our example UI*

If we were successful in grabbing the user's attention in five seconds in the information layout we produced earlier, we don't want to produce something radically different in another aspect of the Watch applications' interface. Here we've repeated the same basic structure from the Glance, the key who, what, when, where, why, and how questions. Around that information we've slotted in additional information for the user. If the user has twenty seconds instead of five, we want to give them the ability to dive a little deeper into the information we have for them. A structure similar to this allows the user to recognize the pattern of information to expect from our application the moment they look at it. The additional details allow the user to capitalize on any additional time they may have to probe us (their assistant) a bit further to find out what else they want to know.

GOING FROM ONE SET OF ANSWERS TO MANY

1. To expand our application's design to show additional details while maintaining a core, recognizable structure we are going to start by setting up the storyboards for our main Watch application (Figure 3.63).

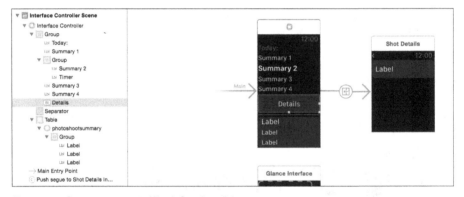

Figure 3.63. Setting up our main Watch Storyboards

2. We'll set up our Interface Controller to use the class InterfaceController. For the row in the table we are going to set the class to PhotoShootSummaryRowController and its identifier to photoshootsummary.

3. For the second interface controller we are going to set it to use the class ShotDetailsInterfaceController. For the row type in its table we are going to set it to use the class ShowInformationRowController, and the identifier shotinformation.

4. For InterfaceController.m, we'll use the following code.

```objc
//
//  InterfaceController.m
//  Chapter6 WatchKit Extension

#import "InterfaceController.h"

#import "Photoshoot.h"

#import "PhotoshootSummarizer.h"
#import "PhotoshootManager.h"

#import "PhotoShootSummaryRowController.h"

@interface InterfaceController()

@property (nonatomic,weak) IBOutlet WKInterfaceLabel *userSummaryLine1;
@property (nonatomic,weak) IBOutlet WKInterfaceLabel *userSummaryLine2;
@property (nonatomic,weak) IBOutlet WKInterfaceTimer
*userSummaryLine2Timer;
@property (nonatomic,weak) IBOutlet WKInterfaceLabel *userSummaryLine3;
@property (nonatomic,weak) IBOutlet WKInterfaceLabel *userSummaryLine4;

@property (nonatomic,weak) IBOutlet WKInterfaceTable *shootListTable;

@property (nonatomic,strong) NSDictionary *userSummaryInformation;

@end


@implementation InterfaceController

- (void)awakeWithContext:(id)context {
    [super awakeWithContext:context];

    [self.userSummaryLine1 setText:@""];
    [self.userSummaryLine2 setText:@""];
    [self.userSummaryLine3 setText:@""];
    [self.userSummaryLine4 setText:@""];
```

```objc
    [self registerForNotifications];
}

- (void)registerForNotifications
{
    [[NSNotificationCenter defaultCenter] addObserver:self selector:@
selector(handleSummaryChange:) name:@"PhotoshootSummaryChanged"
object:nil];
}

- (void)unregisterForNotifications
{
    [[NSNotificationCenter defaultCenter] removeObserver:self];
}

- (void)dealloc
{
    [self unregisterForNotifications];
}

- (void)handleSummaryChange:(NSNotification *)notification
{
    dispatch_async(dispatch_get_main_queue(), ^{
        [self refreshData];
    });
}

- (void)willActivate {
    // This method is called when watch view controller is about to be
visible to user
    [super willActivate];

    [self refreshData];
}

- (void)didDeactivate {
    // This method is called when watch view controller is no longer
visible
    [super didDeactivate];
}
```

```objc
- (void)refreshData
{
    NSArray *photoshoots = [PhotoshootManager photoshoots];
    NSDictionary *userSummary = [PhotoshootSummarizer currentSummaryInf
ormation:photoshoots];

    NSDictionary *lastSummaryInformation = self.userSummaryInformation;

    Photoshoot *mostRelevantShoot = userSummary[@"relevantShoot"];

    NSMutableArray *tempShoots = [photoshoots mutableCopy];
    [tempShoots removeObject:mostRelevantShoot];
    NSArray *otherShoots = [tempShoots copy];

    if (![lastSummaryInformation[@"line1"] isEqualToString:userSummary
[@"line1"]]) {
        [self.userSummaryLine1 setText:userSummary[@"line1"]];
    }

    if (![lastSummaryInformation[@"line2"] isEqualToString:userSummary
[@"line2"]] ||
        ![lastSummaryInformation[@"relevantStart"] isEqualToDate:userSu
mmary[@"relevantStart"]] ||
        ![lastSummaryInformation[@"relevantEnd"] isEqualToDate:userSumm
ary[@"relevantEnd"]] ||
        [lastSummaryInformation[@"onLocation"] boolValue] !=
[userSummary[@"onLocation"] boolValue]) {
        if ([userSummary[@"line2"] isEqualToString:@"#countdown#"]) {
            [self.userSummaryLine2 setHidden:YES];
            [self.userSummaryLine2Timer setHidden:NO];

            if ([userSummary[@"onLocation"] boolValue]) {
                NSDate *relevantDate = userSummary[@"relevantStart"];
                [self.userSummaryLine2Timer setDate:relevantDate];

                [self.userSummaryLine2Timer setTextColor:[UIColor
redColor]];
            } else {
                NSDate *relevantDate = userSummary[@"relevantEnd"];
                [self.userSummaryLine2Timer setDate:relevantDate];
```

```
                    [self.userSummaryLine2Timer setTextColor:[UIColor
whiteColor]];
                }
                [self.userSummaryLine2Timer start];
            } else {
                [self.userSummaryLine2 setHidden:NO];
                [self.userSummaryLine2Timer setHidden:YES];
                [self.userSummaryLine2Timer stop];
                [self.userSummaryLine2 setText:userSummary[@"line2"]];
            }
        }

        if (![lastSummaryInformation[@"line3"] isEqualToString:userSummary
[@"line3"]]) {
            [self.userSummaryLine3 setText:userSummary[@"line3"]];
        }
        if (![lastSummaryInformation[@"line4"] isEqualToString:userSummary
[@"line4"]]) {
            [self.userSummaryLine4 setText:userSummary[@"line4"]];
        }

        self.userSummaryInformation = userSummary;

        [self.shootListTable setNumberOfRows:[otherShoots count] withRowTyp
e:@"photoshootsummary"];

        [otherShoots enumerateObjectsUsingBlock:^(Photoshoot *otherShoot,
NSUInteger idx, BOOL *stop) {
            PhotoShootSummaryRowController *rowController = [self.
shootListTable rowControllerAtIndex:idx];
            [rowController setLocationName:otherShoot.locationName];
            [rowController setProjectDescription:otherShoot.
projectDescription];
            [rowController setRelevantDate:otherShoot.beginTime];
        }];
}

- (id)contextForSegueWithIdentifier:(NSString *)segueIdentifier
{
    if ([segueIdentifier isEqualToString:@"shotInformationSegue"]) {
        Photoshoot *mostRelevantShoot = self.userSummaryInformation[@"
```

```
relevantShoot"];
        NSDictionary *context = @{
            @"shotDetails" : mostRelevantShoot.plannedShots
        };
        return context;
    }

    return nil;
}

@end
```

5. We'll also create the following classes: PhotoShootSummaryRowController, ShotInformationRowController, and ShotDetailsInterfaceController. For those classes we'll use the following code.

```
//
//  PhotoShootSummaryRowController.h
//  Chapter6
//

#import <Foundation/Foundation.h>
#import <WatchKit/WatchKit.h>

@interface PhotoShootSummaryRowController : NSObject

- (void)setLocationName:(NSString *)locationName;
- (void)setProjectDescription:(NSString *)projectDescription;
- (void)setRelevantDate:(NSDate *)relevantDate;

@end

//
//  PhotoShootSummaryRowController.m
//  Chapter6
//

#import "PhotoShootSummaryRowController.h"

@interface PhotoShootSummaryRowController ()

@property (nonatomic,weak) IBOutlet WKInterfaceLabel *locationLabel;
```

```objc
@property (nonatomic,weak) IBOutlet WKInterfaceLabel *projectLabel;
@property (nonatomic,weak) IBOutlet WKInterfaceLabel *dateLabel;

@end

@implementation PhotoShootSummaryRowController


- (void)setLocationName:(NSString *)locationName
{
    [self.locationLabel setText:locationName];
}

- (void)setProjectDescription:(NSString *)projectDescription
{
    [self.projectLabel setText:projectDescription];
}

- (void)setRelevantDate:(NSDate *)relevantDate
{
    [self.dateLabel setText:[relevantDate description]];
}

@end

//
//  ShotInformationRowController.h
//  Chapter6
//

#import <Foundation/Foundation.h>

#import "ShotInformation.h"

@interface ShotInformationRowController : NSObject

- (void)setShotInformation:(ShotInformation *)shotInformation;

@end

//
```

```objc
// ShotInformationRowController.m
// Chapter6
//

#import "ShotInformationRowController.h"

#import <WatchKit/WatchKit.h>

@interface ShotInformationRowController ()

@property (nonatomic,weak) IBOutlet WKInterfaceLabel *shotDescription;

@end

@implementation ShotInformationRowController

- (void)setShotInformation:(ShotInformation *)shotInformation
{
    [self.shotDescription setText:shotInformation.shotDescription];
}

@end

//
// ShotDetailsInterfaceController.h
// Chapter6
//

#import <WatchKit/WatchKit.h>
#import <Foundation/Foundation.h>

@interface ShotDetailsInterfaceController : WKInterfaceController

@end
//
// ShotDetailsInterfaceController.m
// Chapter6
//

#import "ShotDetailsInterfaceController.h"
```

```objc
#import "ShotInformationRowController.h"

@interface ShotDetailsInterfaceController ()

@property (nonatomic,strong) NSArray *shotDetails;

@property (nonatomic,weak) IBOutlet WKInterfaceTable *table;

@end

@implementation ShotDetailsInterfaceController

- (void)awakeWithContext:(id)context {
    [super awakeWithContext:context];

    // Configure interface objects here.
    NSArray *shotDetails = context[@"shotDetails"];
    self.shotDetails = shotDetails;
}

- (void)willActivate {
    // This method is called when watch view controller is about to be
visible to user
    [super willActivate];

    [self updateTable];
}

- (void)didDeactivate {
    // This method is called when watch view controller is no longer
visible
    [super didDeactivate];
}

- (void)updateTable
{
    [self.table setNumberOfRows:[self.shotDetails count] withRowType:@"
shotinformation"];

    for (NSInteger idx = 0; idx < [self.table numberOfRows] && idx <
[self.shotDetails count]; idx++) {
```

```
    ShotInformationRowController *rowController = [self.table
rowControllerAtIndex:idx];

    [rowController setShotInformation:self.shotDetails[idx]];
  }
}

@end
```

6. Additionally, our sample data plist will now look like Figure 3.64.

Key		Type	Value
▼ Root		Dictionary	(1 item)
▼ photoshoots		Array	(3 items)
▼ Item 0		Dictionary	(9 items)
locationBeacon		String	799723ED-3AA3-4FA8-B745-B7EE371F94B1
locationName		String	Acme Design Lab
▼ locationCoordinate		Dictionary	(2 items)
latitude		Number	38.059666
longitude		Number	-97.954506
beginTime		String	2015-06-15T22:30:00Z
endTime		String	2015-06-15T23:30:00Z
shootDescription		String	New Widget Shoot
projectDescription		String	Acme June Campaign
clientContactName		String	Jane Adams
▼ plannedShots		Array	(3 items)
▼ Item 0		Dictionary	(2 items)
shotDescription		String	Shot 1
completed		Boolean	NO
▼ Item 1		Dictionary	(2 items)
shotDescription		String	Shot 2
completed		Boolean	YES
▼ Item 2	○ ⊖	Dictionary	(2 items)
shotDescription		String	Shot 3
completed		Boolean	NO
▼ Item 1		Dictionary	(8 items)
locationBeacon		String	799723ED-3AA3-4FA8-B745-B7EE371F94B1
locationName		String	Walker's Beach
locationCoordinate	○ ⊖	Dictionary ⌃	(2 items)
beginTime		String	2015-06-15T22:30:00Z
endTime		String	2015-06-15T23:30:00Z
shootDescription		String	New Widget Shoot
projectDescription		String	WidgetCo
clientContactName		String	Jane Adams
▼ Item 2		Dictionary	(8 items)
locationBeacon		String	799723ED-3AA3-4FA8-B745-B7EE371F94B1
locationName		String	WidgetMax HDQ
▶ locationCoordinate		Dictionary	(2 items)
beginTime		String	2015-06-15T22:30:00Z
endTime		String	2015-06-15T23:30:00Z
shootDescription		String	New Widget Shoot
projectDescription		String	WidgetMax
clientContactName		String	Jane Adams

Figure 3.64. Sample data plist

7. After these changes we are left with a working application that can quickly grab the user with a familiar structure that they can expect. When they utilize the full application instead of the Glance, they are provided with additional content about future photo shoots they have planned. For the current photo shoot they can dive in another level deeper into the information and see a list of individual shots that have been planned for the photo shoot.

There are still a few items at this point that deviate from our design. These gaps are left as exercises for the reader. Can you modify the example to display friendlier date and time strings for each future photo shoot in its button? Can you display the completed status of individual shots on the shot details interface controller? Can you modify the shot details controller to toggle the completed status of a shot?

Use Notifications as Punctuation

Now that we've worked through our example application, let's put ourselves in the shoes of our photographer's assistant once again. Let's say that our photographer has asked us, as their assistant, to remind them to leave one hour prior to all off-site shoots. As part of our job we would thus interrupt our employer one hour prior to each shoot. With the notifications for a Watch application, this is what we should attempt to model. Our job as the assistant is to provide the most relevant answers to the questions on the mind of the photographer at any point in time. For the times that the photographer isn't actively managing their schedule, it is our job to let them know that something is changing. We need to provide the punctuation as their story is written. We could be providing statements ("Acme Design Lab shoot is in one hour"), questions ("Acme is requesting to move their shoot outdoors. Is that OK?"), or exclamations ("Acme Design Lab shoot is in 30 minutes, current driving time is 45 minutes!"). These interactions map into a Watch or iOS application as notifications. A productive way to think about these are as punctuation within the story you are telling your user. Do you have a statement to make to your user, a question, or an exclamation? These are your notifications, and you need to use them carefully.

Looking Forward: Complications in watchOS 2

If you are familiar with the Apple Watch you've undoubtedly seen Complications on the Watch faces that come with the Apple Watch. These include things like weather, calendar, moon phase, activity, and more (see Figure 3.65).

Figure 3.65. *Moon phase Complication*

Starting with watchOS 2, Complications can also be provided by applications that you make. Despite their name, Complications are a great fit if you find yourself in the situation of needing to tame complex data for an Apple Watch application.

Step back to our initial charge at the beginning of this chapter: how can we take a complex situation and distill it down to a very small area to display to our user. How do we make it relevant? How do we convey the information we need to convey? This becomes even more challenging when you may have a truly small area of a watch face to sum up the entirety of your data to a user. As you move forward with your own Apple Watch application and try to simplify the data you are working with and the story you need to tell your user, I encourage you to frame your thoughts with how the data would be displayed as a Complication. If you can tell a compelling story to your user in that tiny amount of space it becomes much easier to work backwards from there and fill in details as you get a larger and larger amount of area, and larger and larger amount of the user's attention to work with.

Chapter 4

Examining Home Remote and its Components

By Gary Riches, creator of the Home Remote Watch app

Home Remote is a universal iOS app that gives you control of your Internet-connected devices from your Today Screen. It supports a wide range of equipment by mixing native support for certain hardware with the ability to handle generic URLs, which allows you to interface it with any other web service. The iOS app itself allows you to configure the actions that will be displayed on the Today Screen, and the Today Screen extension executes the actions (see Figure 4.1).

Figure 4.1. *The Home Remote Watch app*

The app found moderate success, and requests for a version for the Pebble smart watch started coming through. Interest in wearables was increasing and Apple had already teased the Apple Watch in September of last year. We built the Pebble version in C, keeping the Apple Watch in our minds at all times, and considering how code could be re-used between the Pebble app and possibly what Apple would offer with the WatchKit SDK.

The Today Screen extension is a list of buttons, displayed left to right, top to bottom, and allows paging if there are more actions to display than there is space. This translates very well in to Pebble's equivalent of a UITableView, the MenuLayer and also WatchKit's WKInterfaceTable.

In this chapter we'll create a basic WatchKit app that has a WKInterfaceTable and populates it with data that is shared between the iOS app and the WatchKit extension, similar to the process used in Home Remote.

The WatchKit Extension

Create a new Objective-C, single view application in Xcode called watchkitdemo, noting the Bundle Identifier for later. Once your project is created and open in Xcode, select the project file if it isn't already selected and then, in the right-hand panel, click the "+" to add a new target.

> **Note**   When you see {bundleid} written, substitute your own Bundle Identifier.

You'll be presented with the following dialog box, be sure to select iOS ➤ Apple Watch ➤ WatchKit App, and then click Next.

Figure 4.2. Selecting the WatchKit App as the target

Another dialog box will appear and you can leave all of the default values except for the check box that says Include Notification Glance, which will need to be unchecked. We'll cover adding a glance later in this chapter. Click Finish and you'll see that two new targets have been added; watchkitdemo WatchKit Extension and watchkitdemo WatchKit App, along with corresponding groups in the project navigator that contain the associated classes, storyboards, and plists.

> **Note** Plist, short for Property List, are files that are used to store serialized objects such as user settings.

The User Interface

Click the Interface.storyboard in the watchkitdemo WatchKit App group and you'll see an empty black box. From the utilities panel on the right of the Xcode window, drag a Table component on to your Interface Controller Scene. Finally, drag a label in to the Table Row that is showing.

We'll have to create a class that represents the Table Row Controller that was automatically created for you by Interface Builder as you set the interface up. Right-click the watchkitdemo WatchKit Extension group in the navigator and select New File, then select iOS ➤ Source ➤ Cocoa Touch Class followed by Next. The Class should be named ListTableRowController and be a subclass of NSObject (see Figure 4.3). Click Next and make sure the new file will only be added to the watchkitdemo WatchKit Extension target.

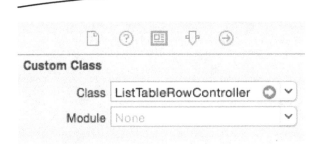

Figure 4.3. Creating the ListTableRowController class

Now that we have the basics of our Watch app display created with their associated classes, we can address the UI components we have just created in exactly the same way using WatchKit as we would for iOS, using IBOutlets.

1. Press the `Show The Assistant Editor` button in Xcode and have the `Interface.storyboard` and `ListTableRowController.h` file both visible.

2. Select the `Table Row Controller` in Interface Builder, and then select the third tab in the utilities panel.

3. In the field where you can type a custom class, type `ListTableRowController`.

4. Select the fourth tab and type `ListTableRowController` for the `Row Controller Identifier`.

5. Select the label you created and select the fifth tab in the utilities panel.

6. Drag a `New Referencing Outlet` from the panel to the `ListTableRowController.h` file that you have open.

7. Call it `name` when prompted.

> **Note** Feel free to set up your IBOutlets in whichever manner you prefer. There are many ways to achieve the same result.

You'll notice that we currently have an error in our code. Xcode is complaining that it doesn't know what a `WKInterfaceLabel` is but thankfully this is easy to resolve, simply import the WatchKit framework with `#import <WatchKit/WatchKit.h>` at the top of your file. We'll also need to provide an IBOutlet for the table we've created so go ahead and repeat these steps, but this time you need to have the `InterfaceController.m` file open instead. Call the IBOutlet `listTable`. With that, our user interface is complete for now.

Populating the Table

Even though the WKInterfaceTable looks quite like a UITableView and behaves quite like a UITableView, unfortunately it isn't coded like a UITableView. Although you will lose the speed that familiarity with an API brings, WatchKit is so basic that it's not hard to pick up and understand the new concepts and APIs. We're going to be using the following to set up and populate our WKInterfaceTable:

- - setNumberOfRows:withRowType: Creates the specified number of row controllers of the same type to use in populating the table with data.

- - table:didSelectRowAtIndex: Called when a user has selected a row in the table by tapping on it.

- - rowControllerAtIndex: Returns the row controller for the row at the specified index in the table.

To start with, let's populate the table with some dummy data. At the top of your InterfaceController.m file, type #import "ListTableRowController.h". Now find the method called awakeWithContext. This is where we will set up the table. First, to set how many rows of information we're going to display, type:

```
[self.listTable setNumberOfRows:10 withRowType:@"ListTableRowController"];

for (int i = 0; i < 10; i++) {

        ListTableRowController *row = [self.listTable
rowControllerAtIndex:i];
        [row.name setText:[NSString stringWithFormat:@"Label: %d", i]];
}
```

Go ahead and test your Watch app on the simulator by choosing the watchkitdemo WatchKit App target and pressing the Build And Run button.

> **Note** If you do not see the Apple Watch simulator, select Hardware
> ➤ External Displays ➤ Apple Watch – 42mm.

You will be able to scroll through the table with the touch screen or the Digital Crown on the side of your Watch. WatchKit handles all of the input automatically.

Handling the Table's Input

Now that our table is populated, we should handle the input. In the case of Home Remote it calls the action associated with the row, but for the purpose of this demo we'll just set up the handler and perform some basic logging to make sure that we are getting the correct values back. We're going to add the method now, but we don't need to set up the delegate of the table as we would do in iOS. The WKInterfaceController that the table resides in will automatically become the delegate for it. Above the awakeWithContext method add:

```
- (void)table:(WKInterfaceTable *)table didSelectRowAtIndex:(NSInteger)
rowIndex{

        NSLog(@"Selected: %ld", (long)rowIndex);
}
```

This method will be called whenever you tap a row in the table and log the number of the row, starting from zero (see Figure 4.4). For the time being we'll leave it at that. Once we have more meaningful data we'll come back to this method and update it.

Figure 4.4. Our example table

Sharing Data Between Extension and App

Since the WatchKit Extension runs as part of a different host application rather than as part of the iOS app, data sharing doesn't occur automatically. You possibly thought that the two would share NSUserDefaults, but this unfortunately isn't the case. Thankfully, Apple has thought of this and adding a shared container for data between the WatchKit Extension and the iOS app is relatively simple.

App Groups

To enable app group data sharing, use Xcode or the Developer portal to enable app groups for the containing app and its contained app extensions.

1. Select the project file in the Project Navigator and, in the central pane, select the `watchkitdemo` target.

2. Click the `Capabilities` tab.

3. Expand the `App Groups` section and switch it to `ON`. After a few seconds the view will change and you will see a "+" allowing you create a new group.

4. Press "+" and enter `group.{bundleid}`.

5. Repeat the process for your watchkitdemo WatchKit Extension.

> **Note** Remember, when you see {bundleid} written, substitute your own Bundle Identifier. Last warning!

iOS

Now that's set up, both your iOS app and WatchKit Extension can create or access an NSUserDefaults suite that they both have read and write access to. Let's write some code to populate it from the iOS app and then read it from the WatchKit Extension to test if it works. In your ViewController.m for iOS, in the viewDidLoad method, add the following code:

```
NSUserDefaults *sharedDefaults = [[NSUserDefaults alloc]
initWithSuiteName:@"group.{bundleid}"];

NSArray *listOfActions =
    @[
    @{@"name": @"Lights On", @"description": @"Turns the lights on"},
    @{@"name": @"Lights Off", @"description": @"Turns the lights off"},
    @{@"name": @"Garage Open", @"description": @"Opens the garage
door"},
    @{@"name": @"Garage Close", @"description": @"Closes the garage
door"}
];

[sharedDefaults setObject:listOfActions forKey:@"listOfActions"];
[sharedDefaults synchronize];

NSLog(@"Done");
```

The code above will load up the NSUserDefaults with the specified suite name. If none exists, it will be created. We create a basic array of dictionaries that will store both a name and a description for each action. In the case of Home Remote we also store a URL and any set up parameters, but looking at human readable data will make the process easier.

Change the run target and run the iOS app. The iOS simulator should load up a white screen and you should see "Done" in the Xcode console pane. The shared defaults that we are going to read in the WatchKit Extension have now been filled. It's now safe to stop that process running by pressing the Stop button in Xcode.

WatchKit

Now we need to read that information into our WatchKit Extension, display it in the table view, and access it when the table is pressed. The process of getting the values out of the shared NSUSerDefaults is almost identical to adding them. Update your awakeWithContext method to look like it is shown below. The parts that have changed are in bold.

```
"- (void)awakeWithContext:(id)context {" )

        [super awakeWithContext:context];

        NSUserDefaults *sharedDefaults = [[NSUserDefaults alloc]
        initWithSuiteName:@"group.{bundleid}"];

        NSArray *listOfActions = [sharedDefaults
objectForKey:@"listOfActions"];

        [self.listTable setNumberOfRows:listOfActions.count
        withRowType:@"ListTableRowController"];

        for (int i = 0; i < listOfActions.count; i++) {
                ListTableRowController *row = [self.listTable
                rowControllerAtIndex:i];
                [row.name setText:listOfActions[i][@"name"]];
        }
}
```

All we've done here is change the hard coded values to instead read from the array length or data. Test the WatchKit app and you'll see that the table reflects the information we entered into the iOS app; it will be showing four rows with the names we set earlier (see Figure 4.5). Now that's all working well, let's do something else when a table row is selected. To do this we'll modify our table:didSelectRowAtIndex method. Update the method to be like this:

```
- (void)table:(WKInterfaceTable *)table didSelectRowAtIndex:(NSInteger)
rowIndex{

    NSUserDefaults *sharedDefaults = [[NSUserDefaults alloc]
    initWithSuiteName:@"group.{bundleid}"];
```

```
    NSArray *listOfActions = [sharedDefaults
objectForKey:@"listOfActions"];

    NSString *selectedActionDescription = listOfActions[rowIndex]
[@"description"];

    NSLog(@"%@", selectedActionDescription);
}
```

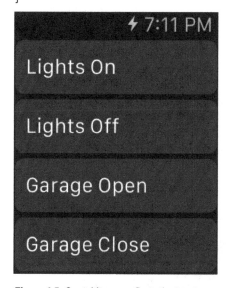

Figure 4.5. Our table now reflects the inputs

We fetch the list of actions from the shared NSUSerDefaults and read the description dictionary value from the array. We make sure we're using the correct array entry by using the `rowIndex` that gets passed into the method.

> **Tip**   You could store a reference to your listOfActions array to avoid getting it each time with the suite name.

You now have a table populated with data from an iOS app, and some WatchKit apps consist of little more than this.

Home Remote is itself just a table that displays data configured from the iOS app, and then calls a URL or sends data to a socket based on the parameters. To take things a little further, try making it look a little nicer by adjusting the label positioning in the row controller to be centered vertically.

Glances and Extension Communication

Launching apps on the Apple Watch can be cumbersome at times, requiring at least a press of the Digital Crown, a swipe of the screen, and then a tap. Apps that offer a glance (the panels of information when you swipe up from a Watch face) can be launched with just a swipe and a tap, which is much faster and more convenient. Apple advises against having a glance in your app just to enable quick launching in their Human Interface Guidelines (HIG), so some thought needs to go into your glance to make it useful.

The Home Remote Glance

The first release of Home Remote didn't include a glance, primarily because it was not obvious that launching the app would become quite arduous after a while, especially for an app that is intended to be launched multiple times per day. This was solved by updating the app and providing a glance that was configurable, just launching the app at its most basic, but offering the option to go right into the voice dictation mode of the app (see Figure 4.6). Here are the two states of the glance for Home Remote for Apple Watch.

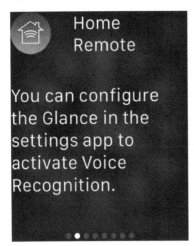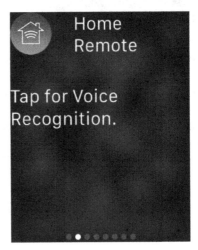

Figure 4.6. The Glance can be used to launch the app in different configurations

For our demo, we'll be pulling a random object from our shared list of actions that we set up, displaying its name and description, and passing that to the WatchKit Extension via Handoff. We have to use Handoff as the glance, although included as part of our WatchKit Extension, Handoff runs separately.

The Glance

Open our project in Xcode and then select your Interface.storyboard from the project navigator. Drag in a Glance Interface Controller from the Object library.

Unlike normal interfaces for WatchKit, glances follow a template-based system. The Apple Watch Human Interface Guidelines offer the following guidance:

"The templates you use to design your glance promote a consistent layout and structure. The upper and lower portions of the glance provide standard baselines for content, and the upper-right corner is reserved for system status indicators. Creating a glance that is inconsistent with other glances may make yours seem out of place and result in the wearer removing it."

To select the template you want to use, select the glance in the Interface Builder navigator and show the attributes inspector (see Figure 4.7). You'll be able to select your templates from there. As we are only showing text, select Body 3 for the top template, and Body 6 as the footer for your lower one.

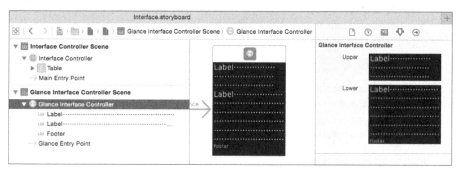

Figure 4.7. This is how your Glance should be configured

> Tip   You can see the name of each template by leaving the mouse pointer hovering over each one. The name will appear in the tooltip.

The labels can have text added manually if the information was going to remain static, but because it's not, we'll have to create a class and assign IBOutlets.

1.   Right-click the watchkitdemo WatchKit Extension group in the project navigator and select New File, then iOS ➤

Source ▶Cocoa Touch Class followed by Next.

2. Name the Class GlanceInterfaceController and make it a subclass of WKInterfaceController.

3. Click Next and make sure the new file will only be added to the watchkitdemo WatchKit Extension target.

4. Go back to your Interface.storyboard and set your Glance Interface Controller's custom class to be the GlanceInterfaceController that we just created. You can do this from the Identity Inspector tab.

5. Press the Show the Assistant editor button in Xcode and have the Interface.storyboard and GlanceInterfaceController.m file both visible.

6. Select the top Label in Interface Builder, and then select the fifth tab in the utilities panel.

7. Drag a New Referencing Outlet from the panel to the GlanceInterfaceController.m file that you have open, and you can call it nameLabel when prompted.

8. Repeat the process for the lower Label and call it descriptionLabel.

9. Finally, select the Footer and either empty it of text, or set it to Hidden.

Open up GlanceInterfaceController.m and in the method called awakeWithContext and change it to be like this:

```
- (void)awakeWithContext:(id)context {
        [super awakeWithContext:context];

    NSUserDefaults *sharedDefaults = [[NSUserDefaults alloc]
    initWithSuiteName:@"group.{bundleid}"];

    NSArray *listOfActions = [sharedDefaults
objectForKey:@"listOfActions"];

    NSUInteger randomIndex = arc4random() % listOfActions.count;

    NSString *selectedActionName = listOfActions[randomIndex][@"name"];
    NSString *selectedActionDescription = listOfActions[randomIndex]
[@"description"];

    [self.nameLabel setText:selectedActionName];
    [self.descriptionLabel setText:selectedActionDescription];
}
```

This code should be familiar by now; we get the shared NSUserDefaults and read the array of actions from it. We then get a random index using the array length and floor() to make sure we're always in bounds. We then read the name and description from the dictionary and set up our labels with the value.

We're all good and ready to test, but you may have noticed that the Apple Watch simulator doesn't have the Watch face app, so we're unable to load glances in the standard way. We'll have to create a scheme instead (see Figure 4.8).

1. Set the active scheme to watchkitdemo WatchKit App.

2. Select Product ➤ Scheme ➤ Edit Scheme A new screen will appear.

3. Press Duplicate Scheme in the bottom left and call it Glance.

4. Select Run in the left hand panel and then Glance in the right-hand panel for the Watch Interface option.

5. After this, press Close.

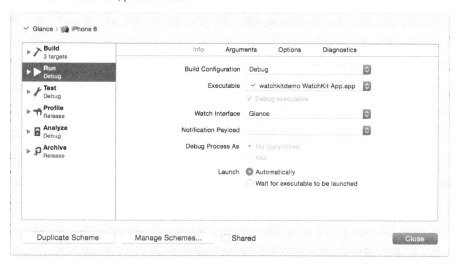

Figure 4.8. The final configuration for the Glance scheme

Run our newly created scheme and you should see our basic, but functioning, glance.

Handoff

As we briefly touched upon earlier, the glance runs independently of the WatchKit Extension, so to let the extension know we have interacted with it via the glance, we need to use the Handoff ability, which is normally associated with moving between devices, such as Apple Watch and iPhone, or iPhone and Mac.

Handoff Interactions

Using a Handoff activity requires three steps:

1.   Create a user activity object in your app.

2.   Set the state of the user activity object with any information you'd like to pass on to another machine or process.

3.   Continue the user activity on a different device when the user requests it.

The Handoff mechanism depends primarily on objects of a single class in Foundation, NSUserActivity. Apps set the information about a user's activities in NSUserActivity object, and those activities can then be continued on other devices or processes.

Upon continuing a Handoff activity on another device or process, the appropriate app is launched and provided with the activity's payload data. A user activity can be continued only in an app that has the same developer Team ID as the activity's source app.

The Handoff Code

We're going to use Handoff just to pass the random number that we create in the glance to the Extension so that we can pull out the same data, but you could pass a reference to a news story, an image, or whatever you require.

Now that the theory is out of the way, let's start adding the code. We're going to be modifying both the WatchKit Extension and the glance. Add the following code to your awakeWithContext method in your GlanceInterfaceController.m:

```
[self updateUserActivity:@"glance.{bundleid}" userInfo:@{@"randomIndex" :
[NSNumber numberWithUnsignedInteger:randomIndex]} webpageURL:nil];
```

The first parameter we pass to the updateUserActivity method is a user-defined string designating the type of activity to be continued. Because we're interacting with a glance here, we prefix the word glance to our Bundle ID. We also pass in an NSDictionary with any pertinent information that we require carrying on the Handoff activity on another device or process. If, at any point, you wanted to cancel the Handoff activity you'd call invalidateUserActivity.

It's a simple task to respond to this from the WatchKit Extension. Add the following code to your InterfaceController.m file:

```
#pragma mark - Handoff -
- (void)handleUserActivity:(NSDictionary *)userInfo
{
    NSUInteger randomIndex = [userInfo[@"randomIndex"]
unsignedIntegerValue];

    NSUserDefaults *sharedDefaults = [[NSUserDefaults alloc]
    initWithSuiteName:@"group.{bundleid}"];
```

```
    NSArray *listOfActions = [sharedDefaults
objectForKey:@"listOfActions"];

    NSString *selectedActionDescription = listOfActions[randomIndex]
[@"description"];
}
```

When the glance opens the main WatchKit Extension it will call this method as part of the Handoff process, passing in the `userInfo` dictionary we created in the glance's call to `updateUserActivity` method. We have to pass the `randomIndex` as an `NSNumber` because an `NSDictionary` can't contain a regular `NSUInteger`. We are now getting the description of the action that was pressed in the glance, but ideally we want to display it somewhere so that we can verify we are using Handoff correctly.

Modal Interface Controllers

To display the selected action that was passed in from Handoff, we'll use a modal interface controller. A modal interface controller is a way to interrupt the current navigation flow temporarily to prompt the user or display other information. It's possible to present a modal interface controller from any interface controller, regardless of the navigation style used by your app, if any. For us to display a modal interface controller we need to do one of the following:

- Create a modal segue in your storyboard file.

- Call the `presentControllerWithName:context:` method to present a single interface controller modally.

- Call the `presentControllerWithNames:contexts:` method to present two or more interface controllers modally using a page based layout.

Because we only want to display just the one modal interface controller, we'll be using `presentControllerWithName:context:` so let's create the class for the modal interface controller and the associated interface.

1. Right-click the `watchkitdemo WatchKit Extension` group in the project navigator and select New File…, then iOS ➤ Source ➤ Cocoa Touch Class followed by Next.

2. The Class should be named `ModalInterfaceController` and be a subclass of WKInterfaceController.

3. Click Next and make sure the new file will only be added to the `watchkitdemo WatchKit Extension` target.

4. Next, open the `Interface.storyboard` and drag a new Interface Controller on the screen, and then set its custom class to be the `ModalInterfaceController` that we

just created.

5.   Finally, drag a label on the new interface controller and connect it up with an IBOulet, calling it `descriptionLabel` and set the number of lines to 0, allowing it to scale.

Your final storyboard should look like Figure 4.9, with our normal interface, the glance, and the one we'll present modally.

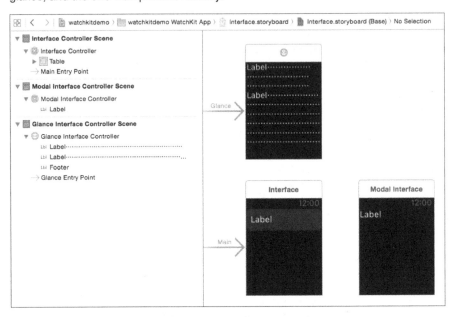

Figure 4.9. *Interface Builder with all of our Interface Controllers assigned*

You may have noticed that `presentControllerWithName:context:` takes a name, and up to now we have not specified one. To remedy this, with the `Modal Interface` selected in Interface Builder, open the Attributes inspector tab and enter `ModalInterfaceController` for the Identifier.

Now that the user interface elements are complete, we'll write the code to make the modal interface controller appear. We'll be calling `presentControllerWithName :context` and passing in our description as the context. The context is type (id) so you can pass whatever your app requires. In your `handleUserActivity:` method in `InterfaceController.m`, at the bottom, add `[self presentControllerWithName:@"Mod alInterfaceController" context:selectedActionDescription];`.

We are able to read this passed value in `awakeWithContext` in `ModalInterfaceController.m`. Edit the method to look like this:

```
- (void)awakeWithContext:(id)context {
    [super awakeWithContext:context];

    [self.descriptionLabel setText:context];
```

}

Test your glance and click on it to advance to the main app. The modal view should now appear, mirroring the description that was on the glance.

We've covered some useful topics in this section. We've learned that Handoff is a powerful way of making sure your glances can show useful information, and that the Watch app can contextually respond to interaction within the glance. Next, we'll look at how other navigation types can be used within the app.

Navigation Types Available

We covered how to add a modal interface controller to our app, but these are only meant to be used if we want to interrupt an existing app flow with an alert, or a small series of questions. But what if we want to show screens of unrelated information, or show hierarchical information such as family, genus, and species of animal? WatchKit has you covered with two different types of navigation for different scenarios.

Here is a summary of the two types of navigation:

- *Page based*. This style is suited for apps with simple data models where the data on each page is not closely related to the data on any other page. A page based interface contains two or more independent interface controllers, only one of which is displayed at any given time. A user can manually swipe between the pages, the page number indicated by the pagination dots at the bottom of the display, or an interface controller can request to become the current page by calling the [self becomeCurrentPage] method.

- *Hierarchical*. This style is suited for apps with more complex data models, or apps whose data is more hierarchical. A hierarchical interface always starts with a single root interface controller. In that interface controller, you provide controls that, when tapped, push new interface controllers onto the screen. An example of this would be if you had a list of animal families, and you wanted to drill down in to the subsequent genus and species.

> **Note** While you cannot have a page based navigation as part of a hierarchical navigation, you can have both types in your app.

Home Remote Navigation

Before the Apple Watch came out, Home Remote used page based navigation. The first page displayed the list of actions you could call, much like our sample application at the moment. The second screen had the voice recognition on it and would launch the Apple Watch voice dictation feature as soon as the screen was displayed. When testing in the simulator, this flow seemed fine, but after testing on the actual Apple Watch I released, this was a sub-optimal implementation. Always test on real hardware if you can, and don't be afraid to throw away what you have if it doesn't work. It's always better to restart earlier than later. Fail fast, don't just keep digging a hole. Figure 4.10 shows the flow of Home Remote before and after the changes.

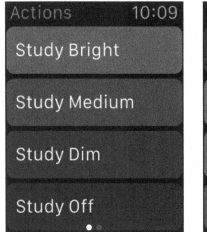 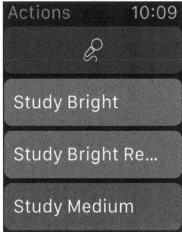

Figure 4.10. A small change in your app can change the usability considerably

You can see that instead of offering a page based solution, a microphone button was added to the top of the list of actions. This took the activation of voice recognition to open app ➤ tap button ➤ speak, rather than open app ➤ swipe ➤ tap button ➤ speak. This improvement, combined with Handoff, allowed you to go directly to voice recognition from tapping the glance. Using real hardware will really help you work out what's best for your app when you make it.

Hierarchy and Page based Navigation

In our test app that we're creating, we so far have our table, the glance, and a modal interface. We're going to add a few different pages to the app now, allowing us to pick either type of navigation type, along with a Force Touch menu that will allow us to restart the choice.

> **Note** Force Touch uses very small electrodes around the display to detect between light and hard presses. It provides instant access to contextually specific controls.

1. Right-click the `watchkitdemo WatchKit Extension` group in the project navigator and select `New File`, then `iOS` ➤ `Source` ➤ `Cocoa Touch Class` followed by `Next`.

2. Name the class `NavigationChoiceInterfaceController` and make it a subclass of WKInterfaceController.

3. Click `Next` and make sure that the new file will only be added to the `watchkitdemo WatchKit Extension` target.

4. Open the `Interface.storyboard` and drag a new `Interface Controller` on to the screen.

5. Set its custom class to be the `NavigationChoiceInterfaceController` that we just created.

6. Drag two buttons on to the new interface and then set their text to be `Page based` and `Hierarchical`.

7. Open the Attributes inspector tab with `NavigationChoiceInterfaceController` selected and set the identifier to `NavigationChoiceInterfaceController`.

We're going to re-use our `ModalInterfaceController` as part of our page based interface, so we should rename it. The refactor tool in Xcode is an easy way of doing this. Open `ModalInterfaceController.h` and double-click the word `ModalInterfaceController` in the line `@interface ModalInterfaceController : WKInterfaceController` and then select Edit ➤ Refactor ➤ Rename.

Xcode will prompt you for a new name, type `DescriptionInterfaceController` and then press `Preview`, followed by `Save`. If Xcode asks you if you want to take automatic snapshots press `Disable`.

> **Note** Refactor will also change your storyboards to use the new class name, but they won't change the Identifier. You should change that for completeness to `DescriptionInterfaceController`.

The starting point of our WatchKit app is going to change to the `Navigation Choice Interface Controller`, and you can define that in Interface Builder.

1. Select the `Navigation Choice Interface Controller` in Interface Builder.

2. Open the Attributes inspector tab.

3. Tick `Is Initial Controller`.

Because we're going to be dynamically adding the original table interface controller in code, we will need to refactor and set the identifier on this interface controller.

Open `InterfaceController.h` and double-click the word `InterfaceController` in the line `@interface InterfaceController : WKInterfaceController,` and then select Edit ➤ Refactor ➤ Rename.

Xcode will prompt you for a new name, type `TableInterfaceController` and then press `Preview`, followed by `Save`. Finally, open the Attributes inspector tab with `TableInterfaceController` selected, and set the identifier to `TableInterfaceController`.

Your final storyboard should look like Figure 4.11.

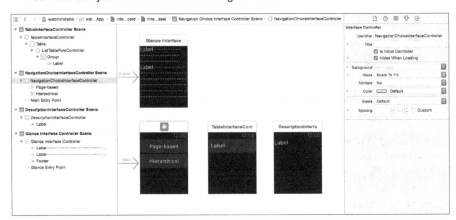

Figure 4.11. *The interface controllers have had their positions changed to better reflect the flow that the app will take*

We're very nearly done with the Interface Builder sections of this chapter and can soon dig in to the code. The last thing we need to do is hook up the buttons we created in the `NavigationChoiceInterfaceController` to the methods they will call. This is done in a very similar way to how we create IBOutlets.

1. In your `Interface.storyboard` select the `Navigation Choice Interface Controller`.

2. Press the `Show the Assistant editor` button in Xcode and

have the Interface.storyboard and NavigationChoiceInte rfaceController.m file both visible.

3. Select the Page based button in the Navigation Choice Interface Controller and then select the fifth tab in the utilities panel, the Connections inspector.

4. Drag a Sent Actions Selector from the panel to the implementation section of your NavigationChoiceInterfa ceController.m file that you have open, and you can call it selectPageBased when prompted.

5. Repeat the process for the Hierarchical button and call it selectHierarchical.

These actions will have created two empty methods ready to be filled with code and should currently look like this:

```
- (IBAction)selectPageBased {
}

- (IBAction)selectHierarchical {
}
```

Page based Navigation

Let's create the selectPageBased method first. We'll go through the code after, but for now type this:

```
- (IBAction)selectPageBased {

    NSMutableArray *pages = [NSMutableArray array];
    NSMutableArray *contexts = [NSMutableArray array];

    NSUserDefaults *sharedDefaults = [[NSUserDefaults alloc]
    initWithSuiteName:@"group.{bundleid}"];

    NSArray *listOfActions = [sharedDefaults
objectForKey:@"listOfActions"];

    for (int i = 0; i < listOfActions.count; i++) {
        NSString *selectedActionDescription = listOfActions[i]
[@"description"];
        [pages addObject:@"DescriptionInterfaceController"];
        [contexts addObject:selectedActionDescription];
    }

        [WKInterfaceController reloadRootControllersWithNames:pages
contexts:contexts];
}
```

First we start by creating two empty arrays; one for the page identifier strings and one for the contexts we pass in to the DescriptionInterfaceController. The code for getting the list of actions should be familiar by now, and after that we loop through the list. For every entry we add a `DescriptionInterfaceController` string along with the description for the action defined at that array entry. We then pass both of these arrays into the method `reloadRootControllersWithNames:contexts`.

> **Note** You may have noticed we call `reloadRootControllersWithNames:contexts` on `WKInterfaceController` rather than on `self`. This is because it is a class method, denoted by the "+" at the beginning of the method signature in the documentation.

We already handled displaying a context in `DescriptionInterfaceController`, so go ahead and test your project. Press the Page based button and you should see what is shown in Figure 4.12.

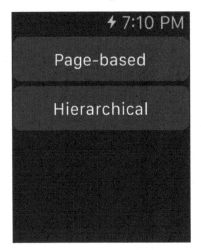

Figure 4.12. We can now swipe from right to left to view the different action descriptions

After pressing the button you'll see a list of all of your action descriptions that you can swipe through easily. One issue we have with this setup is that we have no way of getting back to the main menu without restarting the application. We'll address this issue later in this chapter, but for now, let's get on with hooking up the Hierarchical button.

Hierarchical Navigation

Hierarchical navigation works by pushing interface controllers on to the stack much in the same way that a `UINavigationController` works for iOS. You'll even get the back button in the top left. Change your method to be like this:

```
- (IBAction)selectHierarchical {
    [self pushControllerWithName:@"TableInterfaceController" context:nil];
}
```

We'll also need to update the `table:didSelectRowAtIndex:` method in our `TableInterfaceController.m` to handle pushing a new interface controller onto the screen. We simply need to add the line `[self pushControllerWithName:@"Descrip tionInterfaceController" context:selectedActionDescription];` to the bottom of the method. Build and run the watch app and you'll see that upon pressing the `Hierarchical` button, we can progress from interface controller to interface controller, using the button in the top left or swiping back (see Figure 4.13).

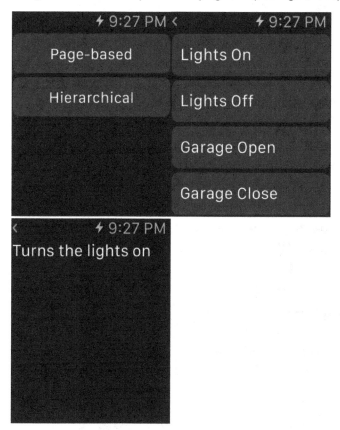

Figure 4.13. The hierarchical flow of the app, from left to right

Great work, but the top of the screen looks a little empty. We can fix that by setting a title for each page. The title is best set in `awakeWithContext:` and is called with `[self setTitle:@"{name}"];`.

1. Set the title for the `NavigationChoiceInterfaceController` to `Menu`.

2.   Set the title for the `TableInterfaceController` to `Actions`.

3.   Set the title for the `DescriptionInterfaceController` to `Info`.

Test your app again and look at the top of the screen. The change should be small, but it's the little details that really finish an app off.

> **Tip**   You can bring your Watch app inline with your brand or iOS app using the Global Tint color. In Interface Builder, open the File inspector tab in the Utilities pane and set the Global Tint color to style your page titles.

Force Touch Menus

Force Touch, found on Apple Watch, provides a new way to interact with content. Instead of just tapping items on the screen, we now have a second form of touch input. Pressing the screen with a small amount of force activates a context menu, if one is defined for the current interface controller. Context menus are optional. You can use them to display actions related to the current screen.

Here are a couple of examples, shown in Figure 4.14, of Force Touch menus from the Mail app and Calendar app on the Apple Watch.

Figure 4.14. The information is always context sensitive and provides a way of having plenty of options available without cluttering the main interface of your Apple Watch app

A context menu is able to display a total of four actions, with each action represented by a string and an image. Tapping an action's image dismisses the menu and calls the method associated with that item. Tapping elsewhere dismisses the menu.

The Design of the Menu Items

Each menu item has an image and a title. The image is different in that it must be a template image, where the alpha channel defines the shape to draw on top of the background. Opaque portions of the image appear as black, and fully or partially transparent portions let the background color show through.

The template images you provide should be smaller than the circular background on which they sit.

> **Tip**   You can learn more about the required sizes and best practices for Apple Watch elements by visiting the Human Interface Guidelines for Apple Watch at https://developer.apple.com/watch/human-interface-guidelines

Apple offers three methods to populate your contextual menu:

```
- (void)addMenuItemWithImage:(UIImage *)image title:(NSString *)title
action:(SEL)action;
```

```
- (void)addMenuItemWithImageNamed:(NSString *)imageName title:(NSString *)
title action:(SEL)action;
```

```
- (void)addMenuItemWithItemIcon:(WKMenuItemIcon)itemIcon title:(NSString *)
title action:(SEL)action;
```

The first, `addMenuItemWithImage:title:action`, is for adding a single image to a menu. You just provide an image, the title and the method to call.

The second is very similar to the first, the only difference being you pass in the name of the image rather than the image itself.

We're interested the third one. Rather than use an image, we'll be using one of the presets that Apple offers, very much like with their default button styles they offer in iOS. The default ones they offer are:

- Accept: a checkmark
- Add: a '+'
- Block: a circle with a slash
- Decline: a 'x'
- Info: an 'i'
- Maybe: a '?'
- More: a '...'

- Mute: a speaker with a slash

- Pause: a pause button

- Play: a play button

- Repeat: looping arrows

- Resume: a circular arrow

- Share: a share icon

- Shuffle: swapped arrows

- Speaker: a speaker icon

- Trash: a trash icon

The context menu is set up in the interface controller where it will be displayed, which for us is the `DescriptionInterfaceController`. Open the file in Xcode and add the following to the bottom of your `awakeWithContext` method:

```
[self addMenuItemWithItemIcon:WKMenuItemIconRepeat
title:@"Restart"
action:@selector(restart)];
```

As you can see from the arguments we pass in, we want the button to show the repeat image. It most matches our requirements, will have the text "Restart," and call a method named `restart`, which we'll create now:

```
- (void)restart {
[WKInterfaceController reloadRootControllersWithNames: @
[@"NavigationChoiceInterfaceController"]
    contexts:nil];
}
```

We simply reload the root interface controller, just as we did to create the page based navigation system, but we only load the `NavigationChoiceInterfaceController`.

Test your app and press the `Page based` button. On the following screen, the `DescriptionInterfaceController`, you can either press and hold the mouse button down if using the simulator, or, if using real hardware, just Force Touch the screen. A menu should appear and look like the one shown in Figure 4.15.

Figure 4.15. *Using Force Touch will bring up this menu*

When you press the button, you should be taken back to the menu choice of whichever navigation style you'd like to see.

Apple Watch Settings

We've seen how some context sensitive menus or settings can be displayed on the Watch using Force Touch, but what about more general settings or configurations? For those we will use WatchKit settings bundles.

The settings you store in your settings bundle are ideally suited to values that change infrequently and that you will use to configure your app's behavior or appearance. The settings bundle is contained inside of your containing iOS app, and the settings themselves are displayed by the Apple Watch app on the user's iPhone.

A WatchKit settings bundle works in the same way as an iOS settings bundle. The settings bundle defines the controls you want displayed by the system and the name of the preference that each control modifies. The Apple Watch app on the user's iPhone takes the settings bundle information and uses it to display the controls to the user. When the user changes the value of a control, the system updates the underlying value.

We're going to add a selection into our settings that will launch the app directly in to one of our navigation types. Let's start by creating our WatchKit settings bundle.

1. Right-click the `watchkitdemo` group in the project navigator and select `New File…`, then iOS ➤ `Apple Watch` ➤ `WatchKit Settings Bundle` followed by `Next`.

2. Name the file `Settings-Watch`.

3. Click Next and make sure that the new file will only be
    added to the watchkitdemo target, and then click Create.

In your project navigator you'll see the Settings-Watch.bundle with a small arrow
next to it. Click the arrow to show the settings bundle contents and then click on the
Root.plist.

> **Note** We must add the WatchKit Settings Bundle to the main target
> because although the settings are for the Watch, they are displayed
> in the Apple Watch iOS app.

Your plist file will be populated with some examples already. Delete everything
under the Preference Items group, then select the empty group and click the "+" icon.
A menu will appear and you should select Multi Value from the list. Set it up so that it
mirrors what is shown in Figure 4.16.

Key	Type	Value
⧉ < > watchkitdemo > watchkitdemo > Settings-Watch.bundle > Root.plist > No Selection		
Key	Type	Value
▼ iPhone Settings Schema	Dictionary	(3 items)
Strings Filename ⇕ ⊕ ⊖	String	Root
▼ Preference Items ⇕	Array	(1 item)
▼ Item 0 (Multi Value - Menu Style)	Dictionary	(6 items)
Type ⇕	String	Multi Value
Title ⇕	String	Menu Style
Identifier ⇕	String	menuStyle
Default Value ⇕	String	0
▼ Titles ⇕	Array	(3 items)
Item 0	String	Default
Item 1	String	Page-based
Item 2	String	Hierarchical
▼ Values ⇕	Array	(3 items)
Item 0	String	0
Item 1	String	1
Item 2	String	2
ApplicationGroupContainerIdentifier ⇕	String	group.mobi.bouncingball.watchkitdemo

Figure 4.16. Plist files are a way of configuring the settings for your iOS and Apple Watch apps

You will see from the plist configuration that we have three items listed: Default,
Page based and Hierarchical with corresponding values of 0, 1 and 2. Also important
to note is the ApplicationGroupContainerIdentifier field that has a value of group.
{bundleid}. This is because the settings bundle resides within the iOS app itself, so
it will need to use the application group's capabilities to share the data between the
application and the associated extension.

Go ahead and test your WatchKit application. After it has opened, select the Apple
Watch app on your iOS device of the iOS simulator, and then select watchkitdemo. You
should see an entry titled Menu Style. Tap it, select Hierarchical and then back out
of the menu. We can read this value from out of our shared NSUserDefaults in the

app. To do this, edit the `awakeWithContext` method in your `NavigationChoiceInterfa ceController.m` to look like this:

```
- (void)awakeWithContext:(id)context {
[super awakeWithContext:context];

[self setTitle:@"Menu"];

NSUserDefaults *sharedDefaults = [[NSUserDefaults alloc]
initWithSuiteName:@"group.mobi.bouncingball.watchkitdemo"];

int menuStyle = [[sharedDefaults objectForKey:@"menuStyle"] intValue];

if (menuStyle == 1) {
    [self selectPageBased];
} else if (menuStyle == 2) {
    [self selectHierarchical];
}
}
```

You know the shared settings code by now so we'll skip over that. The new code is fetching the value of our menu settings and then just calling the methods we assigned to our menu choice buttons before. Go ahead and change that value, and then re-launch the app. You will see the menu choice reflected.

> **Note**   If you're testing the app on an Apple Watch you may have to quit the Watch app and re-launch it to see the change.

We've covered a lot of the building blocks of WatchKit apps now. You should hopefully be getting a feel for what it takes to tie all of the different components together by now. The keen-eyed among you may have noticed we've broken our glance during the refactor. We'll address that next by modifying our app to accept voice input for selecting the navigation type, and provide customization options to configure the glance.

Home Remote and Voice Recognition

Due to the limited nature of input on the Apple Watch, voice input is becoming an increasingly used method of input. From Siri, which can be activated without any button presses, to textual input via speech, voice is the most commonly used method of input for messaging on the Apple Watch. Because of this, it made sense to have voice recognition in the launch version of Home Remote. As the app was available for launch, all development had been done on the simulator. Without having the hardware in-hand, it was decided to use a page based navigation; the first page being the list of actions and the second page being the launcher for voice recognition.

While this worked well on the simulator, on actual hardware it felt cumbersome and unwieldy. It was decided, based on customer feedback, that the voice recognition be moved to a button that sits with the actions you can call, bringing the app all on one screen (see Figure 4.17). The app flow then became: launch app ➤ tap voice recognition button ➤ speak ➤ tap Done. Once this functionality was complete it became very easy to tie that functionality in to the glance that we had created, so the flow became: Tap glance ➤ speak ➤ tap Done. This made the app feel much more responsive, something that is required with the current way Apple has the Watch Extension on the phone.

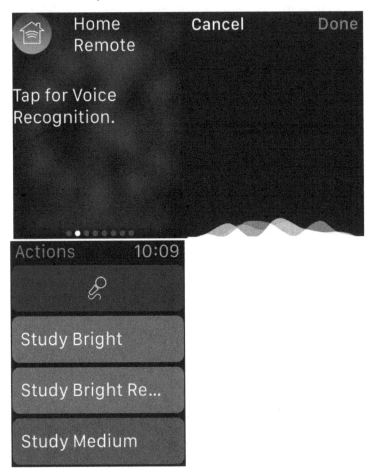

Figure 4.17. The flow of Home Remote after adding the configurable Glance for voice recognition

About Voice Dictation

WatchKit provides the modal interface for using voice dictation as text input. When presented, the interface allows the user to enter text via dictation, or to select from a standard set of phrases or emoji. The interface is presented by calling the method `presentTextInputControllerWithSuggestions: allowedInputMode: completion:`. Let's look at the types of arguments you can provide:

- `presentTextInputControllerWithSuggestions:` The first parameter is an NSArray of possible options you can present the user with on the voice dictation screen. For Home Remote we already have a list of options on the screen before the voice dictation so we pass in `nil`. As the simulator doesn't support voice dictation, you'll need to pass in something if you're using it.

- `allowedInputMode:` The type of input to allow, this can be either plain, plain with emojis, or plain with animated emojis. For our sample app we'll be using plain.

- `Completion:` An array that contains the voice input from the user, or nil if the voice dictation was cancelled. The result of voice dictation is an array rather than a string so as to provide support for returning an NSData object for any emojis that were used in the message.

Adding Voice Recognition to the Table

First things first, let's start by adding a voice recognition button to our `TableInterfaceController.m` file. This button will instantiate an instance of the in-built `TextInputController` and wait for input from the user (see Figure 4.18).

Open the `Interface.storyboard` in Interface Builder and then select the `NavigationChoiceInterfaceController` scene from the `Document Outline` pane. Drag a button from the `Object library` and place it below the two existing ones. Set its text to `Voice`. The final interface should look like this.

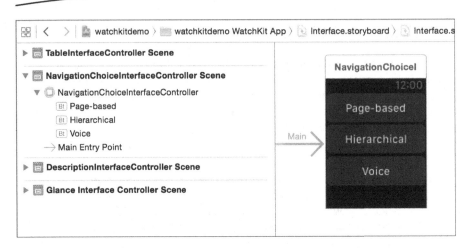

Figure 4.18. *Creating and connecting the Voice button to use the Apple Watch voice recognition functionality*

Finally, we need to hook up the buttons to the methods that they will call.

1. Press the `Show the Assistant editor` button in Xcode and have the `Interface.storyboard` and `NavigationChoiceInterfaceController.m` file both visible.

2. Select the `Voice` button in the `Navigation Choice Interface Controller` and then select the fifth tab in the utilities panel, the Connections inspector.

3. Drag a `Sent Actions Selector` from the panel to the implementation section of your `NavigationChoiceInterfaceController.m` file that you have open, and call it `selectVoice` when prompted.

Now that our button is hooked up to the `selectVoice` method, we'll need to add the following code:

```objc
- (IBAction)selectVoice {

    [self presentTextInputControllerWithSuggestions:nil
allowedInputMode:WKTextInputModePlain
completion:^(NSArray *results) {

        if (results != nil) {

            NSString *dictation = [results[0] lowercaseString];

            if ([dictation isEqualToString:@"page based"]) {
                [self selectPageBased];
```

```
        } else if ([dictation isEqualToString:@"hierarchical"]) {
            [self selectHierarchical];
        }
    }
}];
}
```

There's quite a lot there so let's go through it line by line. The first method called is presentTextInputControllerWithSuggestions, passing in nil for the suggestions. If you're using the simulator then you will need to pass in an array of strings. The array, @[@"page based", @"hierarchical"], instead of nil will work.

We are also passing in WKTextInputModePlain for the allowedInputMode. This means that no emojis, animated or otherwise, will be permitted.

Finally, we define the completion block of the presentTextInputControllerWithSuggestions method.

- We check if the array of results is not nil. This would be the case if the action was cancelled.

- We get the first results of the array. There would only be multiple results if we allowed using emojis.

- We convert the string to lowercase. This is always good practice if comparing strings.

- We see if the dictated text matched the words "page based," and if so, we call the selectPageBased method.

- If not, we see if the dictated text matched the word "hierarchical," and if so, we call the selectHierarchical method.

Go to your app's settings on the Apple Watch app and set the Menu Style back to Default, and then test your Watch app. Press the Voice button and dictate the words "page based" or "hierarchical" (pronounced hire-ark-ick-all) followed by pressing Done. Your app should call the associated method and change the navigation style.

> **Note** Blocks, like the one we used here, are an incredibly powerful, and useful, tool. You can read more about them here: https://developer.apple.com/library/ios/documentation/Cocoa/Conceptual/ProgrammingWithObjectiveC/WorkingwithBlocks/WorkingwithBlocks.html.

Modifying the Settings and Glance

You may feel that there are too many steps to changing the navigation type using voice, similar to Home Remote. We're going to add a new setting to our WatchKit bundle that will enable us to configure the glance to launch right in to the voice dictation interface controller. To start with, we'll add the setting into the settings bundle.

1. Open the `Root.plist` inside of the `Settings-Watch.bundle`.

2. Select `Preference` Items and click the "+".

3. Select `Toggle Switch` from the drop-down menu.

4. Set the Title to Voice for Glance.

5. Finally, set the `Identifier` to `voiceForGlance`.

We'll be reading that value in our `GlanceInterfaceController.m` to establish what text we should display. Open the `GlanceInterfaceController.m` and change the awakeWithContext to be like the following:

```
- (void)awakeWithContext:(id)context {
    [super awakeWithContext:context];

    NSUserDefaults *sharedDefaults = [[NSUserDefaults alloc]
                                        initWithSuiteName:@"group.
mobi.bouncingball.watchkitdemo"];

    NSArray *listOfActions = [sharedDefaults
objectForKey:@"listOfActions"];

    NSUInteger randomIndex = arc4random() % listOfActions.count;

    NSString *selectedActionName = listOfActions[randomIndex][@"name"];
    NSString *selectedActionDescription = listOfActions[randomIndex]
[@"description"];

    if ([sharedDefaults boolForKey:@"voiceForGlance"]) {
        [self.nameLabel setText:@"Voice Recognition"];
        [self.descriptionLabel setText:@"Tap to start"];

        [self updateUserActivity:@"glance.mobi.bouncingball.watchkitdemo"
userInfo:@{@"voiceRecognition" : [NSNumber numberWithBool:TRUE]}
webpageURL:nil];
    } else {
        [self.nameLabel setText:selectedActionName];
        [self.descriptionLabel setText:selectedActionDescription];

        [self updateUserActivity:@"glance.mobi.bouncingball.watchkitdemo"
userInfo:@{@"randomIndex" : [NSNumber numberWithUnsignedInteger:randomInd
ex]}
webpageURL:nil];
    }
}
```

You'll see that only the bottom of the method has changed, where we check for the boolean value of the voiceForGlance key we have in our settings. We can re-purpose the two labels we already have for the text. Also, if we're using voice recognition, we update the userInfo dictionary we pass in to the updatedUserActivity that gets used in Handoff.

Now we just need to read the values in the userInfo and establish whether the app was activated from the voice recognition glance, or the more general one. We previously handled the glance Handoff in our TableInterfaceController.m with the handleUserActivity method. We'll need to move that code now to our first Interface Controller, so cut the whole method from the TableInterfaceController.m and paste it into the NavigationChoiceInterfaceController.m. Because we now have a choice of two different actions that we can perform, we'll add an if statement in there:

```
- (void)handleUserActivity:(NSDictionary *)userInfo
{
    if ([userInfo[@"voiceRecognition"] boolValue]) {
        [self selectVoice];
    } else {
        NSUInteger randomIndex = [userInfo[@"randomIndex"]
unsignedIntegerValue];

        NSUserDefaults *sharedDefaults = [[NSUserDefaults alloc]
        initWithSuiteName:@"group.mobi.bouncingball.watchkitdemo"];

        NSArray *listOfActions = [sharedDefaults
objectForKey:@"listOfActions"];

    NSString *selectedActionDescription =
    listOfActions[randomIndex][@"description"];

        [self presentControllerWithName:@"ModalInterfaceController"
context:selectedActionDescription];
    }
}
```

We can hook in to our existing method, selectVoice, so there are very few lines to change. Give your app a test, configure the glance in settings, and then launch the app from it. You'll briefly see the navigation choice menu and then the app will bring up the voice dictation screen.

You've now been exposed to many different WatchKit topics, and are hopefully thinking about your own Apple Watch app. Remember to test on real hardware where possible, be as creative as you can, and don't be afraid to fail. Now le'ts go over what you'll need to do to submit your new app.

Submitting Your App for Review

Now that your app is completed and you've tested it on hardware, it is time to submit it to Apple. This section will guide you through the submission process, adding screenshots and some of the common "gotchas" that you might come across.

App Identifiers

Your iOS app, Apple Watch App and Apple Watch Extension all need their own unique App Identifiers. These can be configured in the iOS Developer Center. You can also create the provisioning files for them here or let Xcode handle that automatically – if it throws an error just select Fix Issue in the dialogue that appears.

Version Numbers

In our sample project we have three targets. In a real project you might have even more, such as a Today Screen extension. When submitting your app to Apple, you must make sure that your version and build numbers match across all targets. If they don't match you'll still be able to archive the app, but the submission process will fail, which is a real time waster, especially if the app is a large one.

You can edit the values of the version and build numbers in the General tab of each target, or in the Info.plist of each target.

App Name and Settings Name

Our app name when installed on the iOS device and in the Apple Watch app settings has so far been watchkitdemo. This doesn't have a great ring to it.

To change the name displayed on the screen and in the settings, select the Info tab of the iOS app's target, and change the Bundle name field to something you like (see Figure 4.19).

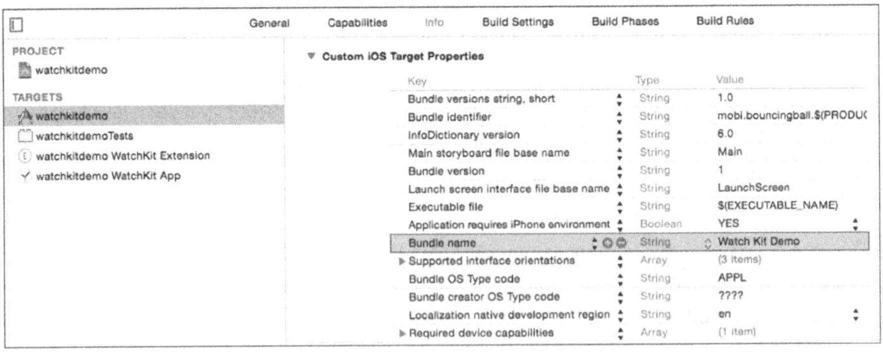

	General	Capabilities	Info	Build Settings	Build Phases	Build Rules

Key	Type	Value
Bundle versions string, short	String	1.0
Bundle identifier	String	mobi.bouncingball.$(PRODUC
InfoDictionary version	String	6.0
Main storyboard file base name	String	Main
Bundle version	String	1
Launch screen interface file base name	String	LaunchScreen
Executable file	String	$(EXECUTABLE_NAME)
Application requires iPhone environment	Boolean	YES
Bundle name	String	Watch Kit Demo
▶ Supported interface orientations	Array	(3 Items)
Bundle OS Type code	String	APPL
Bundle creator OS Type code	String	????
Localization native development region	String	en
▶ Required device capabilities	Array	(1 item)

PROJECT
watchkitdemo

TARGETS
watchkitdemo
watchkitdemoTests
watchkitdemo WatchKit Extension
watchkitdemo WatchKit App

▼ Custom iOS Target Properties

Figure 4.19. The Bundle name is the name your app will display to users on the iOS device home screen or the Watch settings

Note If you don't see the name change reflected on the app or in the settings app, delete the app from the device and reinstall it.

Assets Required for Submission

You should keep your WatchKit app icon visually similar to your iOS app icon to show users that they are connected. All icons should be square, with no transparency. iOS will apply the circular mask. There are many different size requirements for different instances of your Apple Watch icon, so it's recommended to use something such as a template to generate all of the icons and name them. One such example is the Apple Watch App Icon Template at http://appicontemplate.com/watch (see Figure 4.20).

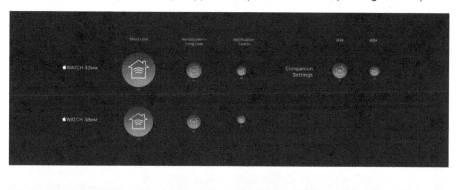

Figure 4.20. The Apple Watch App Icon Template by Danish designer Michael Flarup is a real time saver

Screen Shots

You can upload up to five screenshots of your Apple Watch app. They should be 312 x 390 pixels and have no transparency. Use the full space for the screenshot. Do not frame the screenshot in an Apple Watch. You should also avoid placing your Apple Watch app within your iPhone app screenshots.

Two screenshots are initially visible in the screenshot carousel, so those should feature the best parts of your app.

> **Note** You can take a screenshot of your Apple Watch in the Apple Watch simulator by pressing Command + S. If you are using an Apple Watch you can press the Digital Crown and the side button at the same time. The screenshot will appear in your Photos app.

The Submission Process

When you're finally ready to submit your app to iTunes Connect for review, set the active scheme to be your main iOS app. Make sure either your connected device or iOS Device is selected in the active scheme too.

From the top menu select Product ➤ Archive. After the app has compiled, which may take a little while, you'll be presented with the Organizer window and your app's archive (see Figure 4.21).

Figure 4.21. From the iOS organizer you can submit, validate or export your app

Press the Submit to App Store button and then select your Development Team from the drop-down menu that has appeared. You'll have a final opportunity to check the signing and entitlements on everything before pressing the final Submit button (see Figure 4.22).

Figure 4.22. The profiles used to sign your app will be shown here

After pressing `Submit`, Xcode will build the package to send to iTunes Connect and notify you if it was a success or a failure. Be sure to read any warnings that you get back. They may only be warnings rather than errors but should normally be addressed if possible. Ideally, you'll see the sweet submission successful screen shown in Figure 4.23.

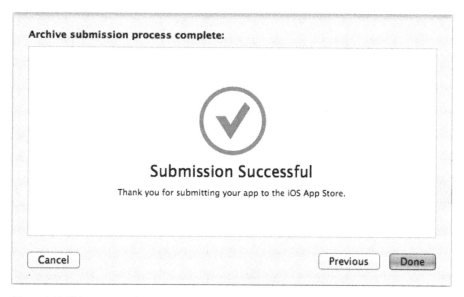

Figure 4.23. This screen is when you crack open your beverage of choice, sit back and bask in your glory

Now that the build has gone to iTunes Connect, you need to head on over there and depending on whether it's a new app or an update, complete the final steps.

Summary

That's it! You've gone through all of the steps from building an app to submitting it. After spending so much time building your app, don't throw it all away:

- Take the time to prepare nice screenshots. Sites like http://launchkit.io/ can really help.

- Spend some time on your app's copy. If you feel you're not up to the job, then getting a professionally written app description isn't as expensive as you'd think.

- Make sure your icon is visually appealing. A lot of people only look at the icon and first two screenshots.

Best of luck in your apps, and I'd be super keen to see them. You can find me on Twitter for any questions, information or help, I'm @Gary_BBGames.

Chapter 5

Developing Notation – Audio to Musical Score

By Jamie Maison, creator of the Notation Watch app

When the Apple Watch was released, it became apparent that the device would allow users to perform specific tasks far quicker than they ever could on the iPhone. It was with this in mind that I decided to create an Apple Watch version of my application Notation, which converts the regular audio from your iPhone's microphone into musical score and guitar TAB.

The idea behind Notation in the first place was to bring a tool to the hands of musicians that takes the unnecessary complications out of writing music, leaving the user to focus solely on the content. So when the opportunity came to allow users to detect notes even quicker than they could before using the Apple Watch, I decided to get to work making this a reality. Today the Apple Watch version allows users to detect individual notes, right on their wrists, both easier and quicker than ever before.

This chapter looks to outline some of the various features that make up Notation, talking about the problems faced in the development of the Apple Watch application and how I overcame them. To start with I will outline how to go about setting out your user interface while including a few workarounds for common problems. I will then outline how some of the core functionality is processed within the Apple Watch application.

User Interface on the Apple Watch

The very first thing that users will ever notice about your Apple Watch application is the user interface. It is arguably the most important aspect of creating a good impression of your application. In this section we will look to analyze some important things to remember when creating user interfaces on the Apple Watch, as well as looking at some solutions to common challenges you might face.

When creating user interfaces for Apple Watch, Xcode fundamentally behaves in a different way compared to that of the iPhone or iPad. You may be used to placing elements of your UI wherever you desire ordinarily, however Xcode makes use of what Apple calls "groups," which are essentially containers for sets of elements. Groups have a few benefits such as:

- Allowing users to easily arrange elements horizontally or vertically in their view.

- They can be placed inside of each other allowing for easy management of more complex layouts.

- They have a number of settings that can be configured via the Attributes Inspector such as layout, background image, and positioning. These setting can be especially useful for a number of reasons; we'll talk more about those in a second.

When WatchKit was first introduced, many developers were apprehensive to the changes that Apple made to the way user interfaces were constructed. In particular, many felt that not being able to stack elements on top of each other hindered the design and feel of their UI. There is, however, one solution that is easy to implement that allows developers to stack images on top of each other, and it uses the "groups" that we talked about earlier.

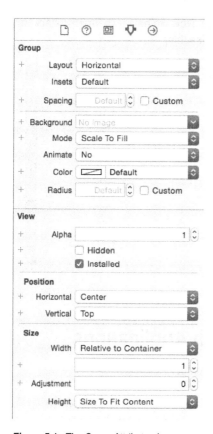

Figure 5.1. The Group Attributes Inspector

USING GROUPS TO STACK UI IMAGES

1. Open your application's Apple Watch Interface.storyboard and place within it a group by dragging it onto your storyboard from the object library (see Figure 5.2).

2. Inside that group, add an Image object. This will hold the image that you want to be foremost in the stack. To select which image you want to display, simply type the image name in the section marked appropriately, "Image."

For the image that you want to be behind the image that you just placed, click the group we created earlier in the document outline and click the icon to bring up the Attributes Inspector. Look for the section that says "Background" and type in the name of the image you want to be the background image. Now we have two images stacked on top of each other and your screen should look like this.

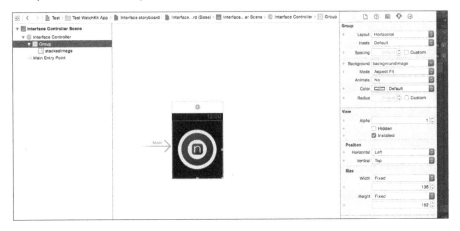

Figure 5.2. *Finished stacked images*

Branding Within Apple Watch Applications

Apple's Human Interface Guidelines state that developers should:

Avoid displaying your logo in your app. Space is limited. Use that space for content, not for non-functional branding elements.

Apple's guidelines have always been there to help developers create the best looking applications possible and I certainly agree that space is at a premium on the Apple Watch, particularly with the 38mm version. However, in my opinion, branding is fundamental in order to promote sales of your application so when designing Notation, I made a conscious decision to find a way to include my branding in the Apple Watch application.

The solution I came up with is fairly simple but allows users to see the Notation logo without taking up valuable space. To achieve this, when Notation on the Apple Watch loads, the Image has a default image of the Notation logo. However when Notation detects its first note, the UIImage is hidden and is instead replaced with the note that was just found. The code behind this function looks like this:

```
if(noteValue >= 42 && noteValue < 78) {
      _notationLogo.hidden = YES;
      _noteImage.hidden = NO;
   }
```

Here we see that if the note value goes between 42 or 78 (our lowest and highest notes) then the Notation Logo is hidden and the note image is unhidden, thus including the application's branding without taking up valuable space.

Other ways you may include branding may be:

- Making your logo disappear on a button press or after a certain amount of time.

- Using your brand's color as the global tint color of your application.

- Using transitions to segue from your brand to the main content.

- Alternatively, include all of your branding on your companion iPhone application.

Design Considerations

There is no doubting that the design of an application plays a large part in whether it is successful or not. Coming up with a good looking and intuitive design can't always be easy, however there are a few things you can keep in mind that will help you create a great looking application as well as a functional one.

- Remember that space on the Apple Watch is at a premium. We want to fill the screen with useful elements. If it doesn't perform a function or have a use, try not to include it.

- Try and lay out buttons the full width of the screen. With the width of the Apple Watch in mind, the UI will always look cleaner if you do not cram too many elements side by side. At the very most only use two or three buttons side by side.

- Consider making the background of your application black. The Apple Watch's bezel is black and having a black background will ensure that there is a seamless transition between the Watch and the application, which is altogether more aesthetically pleasing.

- Use negative space effectively. Blank space can lend itself really well to UI design because it leaves the content to stand out and be altogether more noticeable.

- Consider using color to help users differentiate between elements in your application. If all of your text is the same color, users may find it hard to initially navigate around your application. Try changing the text color of certain elements to help differentiate them from others.

Working with App Groups

When Apple announced that the Apple Watch would support native development at WWDC in June 2015, it meant that developers could finally break free from being tethered to the iPhone and create watchOS apps that ran by themselves. It is important to note, however, that in certain circumstances it would be beneficial for the bulk of an Apple Watch application's processing to be done on the iPhone instead of the Apple Watch target. Fundamentally, the iPhone is a much more powerful device than the Apple Watch and your application will perform faster (and more accurately) if some of the more complex tasks where processed on the iPhone.

With this in mind you may be wondering: how can a developer then transfer information between the iPhone and the Apple Watch? In this chapter we will explore using a capability that Apple calls App Groups that will allow you to communicate between your iPhone and Apple Watch device.

What are App Groups?

Despite your Apple Watch application being nestled within your application project, the two targets have no way of accessing each other's information, and this is where App Groups come into play. Once enabled, App Groups allow developers to share information between application extensions and its parent application.

Setting Up App Groups in Your Project

The first step when using App Groups to transfer data between one another is enabling the App Group capability in both your extension and your containing app. To do this, first you must open Xcode and navigate to the Capabilities tab of your containing application. Next, scroll down to the App Groups section and switch it from OFF to ON (shown in Figure 5.3). You then need to choose your development team from the drop-down menu. Once selected this will add the App Groups entitlement to your Apple App ID.

Figure 5.3. The App Groups switch

The next step is to click the "+" icon and name your App Group. It must be in the format group.company.name. As an example for Notation we used group.notation. applewatch (See Figure 5.4). Once you've chosen a name, click OK and you've successfully completed the first part of the setup!

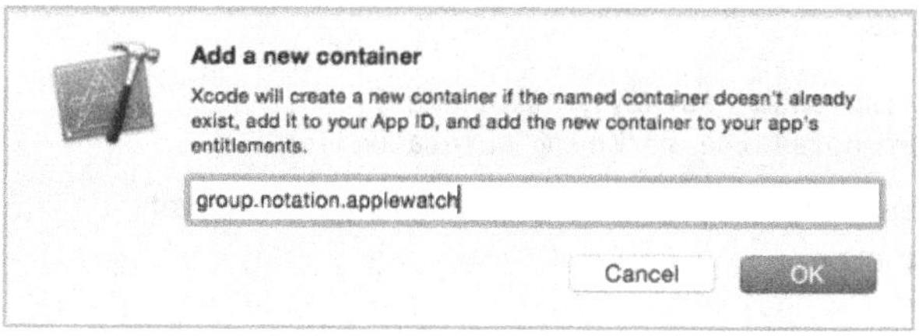

Figure 5.4. Choosing a name

The next step is to repeat the process above for your Apple Watch extension target. This time you won't have to click the "+" symbol to create a new group because we have already created one. Instead simply ensure that the box next to your previously created group is ticked.

Figure 5.5. This is how your App Groups section should look now

That is it for the setup part, now you have a fully functioning App Group set up and you can use it to transfer all manner of information between your WatchKit application and your containing application.

STORING INFORMATION WITH APP GROUPS

We now have an App Group set up, but it is not much good to us without knowing how to use it.

If you are at all familiar with using NSUserDefaults within your standard iPhone application development, you'll be pleased to know that there is very little difference between the code you are familiar and the code within your Apple Watch extension. Principally they are the same, however instead of using standardUserDefaults you now are using your App Group. There are three steps to storing data into your App Group:

1.   First you must create your NSUserDefaults object.

```
NSUserDefaults *notationAppGroup = [[NSUserDefaults alloc]
initWithSuiteName: @"group.notation.applewatch"];
```

2.   Now you can store your data and assign it a key. Think of keys as unique identifiers that allow your app to understand what data you

would like to access.

```
[notationAppGroup setObject:noteName forKey:@"noteName"];
[notationAppGroup setInteger:noteValue forKey:@"noteValue"];
```

3. It is important to synchronize your NSUserDefaults App Group at the end of your function.

```
[notationAppGroup synchronize];
```

RETRIEVING INFORMATION WITH APP GROUPS

Now you have saved your data to your App Group and it is available universally across your container application and your WatchKit application, but how can we access this data?

1. As before, create your NSUserDefaults object.

```
NSUserDefaults *notationAppGroup = [[NSUserDefaults alloc]
initWithSuiteName: @"group.notation.applewatch"];
```

2. Retrieve your data by using the relevant key that we set earlier.

```
NSString *noteName = [defaults objectForKey:@"noteName"];
int noteValue = [notationAppGroup integerForKey:@"noteValue"];
```

And there we have it! You can use your App Group to store all sorts of data, strings, integers, images, etc.

Using the Apple Watch Microphone in watchOS 2

Since the announcement of native Apple Watch support at WWDC in June 2015, developers are now able to work with the hardware available in the device itself. This means that developers can now access the Apple Watch's microphone. In this section we will run through how to use the device's microphone using both Swift and Objective-C.

The first step in using the Apple Watch's microphone is to create a file where a recording will be stored. This is neccesary so that the app knows where to store the audio information produced by the microphone. Currently you can store the recording in the following formats:

■   .wav – An uncompressed format that allows for near-lossless audio quality.

■   .mp4 – A compressed format that allows for smaller file sizes but a decrease in quality.

■   .m4a – Almost identical to an .mp4 however an .m4a is the default format recognised by Apple devices and iTunes.

In order to set the path where the recording will be stored, you create a file URL using NSURL.

```
    NSArray *filePaths = NSSearchPathForDirectoriesInDomains(NSDocumentDire
ctory,

NSUserDomainMask,YES);
    NSString *path = [[filePaths firstObject] stringByAppendingPathComponen
t:@"recording.wav"];
    NSURL *fileUrl = [NSURL fileURLWithPath:path];
```

Because you have now set the NSURL where your recording is to be saved within your application, you can move on to calling the method that requests access to the Watch's microphone. You do this as follows.

Swift

```
self.presentAudioRecordingControllerWithOutputURL(
            self.recFileURL(),
            preset: WKAudioRecordingPreset.HighQualityAudio,
            maximumDuration: 5.0,
            actionTitle: "SomeTitle") { (didSave, error) -> Void in
        }
```

Objective-C

```
[self presentAudioRecordingControllerWithOutputURL:fileUrl
        preset:WKAudioRecording
        PresetHighQualityAudio
        maximumDuration:5.0
        actionTitle:@"Title"
        completion:^(BOOL
        didSave, NSError * __nullable error) {
}];
```

It is important to note that there are three presets in which you can choose, which are WKAudioRecordingPresetHighQualityAudio, WKAudioRecordingPresetWideBandSpeech, and WKAudioRecordingPresetNarrowBandSpeech, which have their own benefits:

- WKAudioRecordingPresetHighQualityAudio – For high fidelity audio applications whereby you want to keep as much quality as possible.

- WKAudioRecordingPresetWideBandSpeech – Allows for a wide band permitting the capture of speech across a wider frequency spectrum.

- WKAudioRecordingPresetNarrowBandSpeech – Has a narrow frequency band allowing for more precise speech recordings.

You can now use the Apple Watch's microphone for audio purposes without the need of relying on the iPhone's microphone. It is important to note however that the iPhone has a much more accurate microphone so it may be necessary to keep that in mind when creating audio applications!

Translating Audio Data into Visual Information

So far we've learned how to transfer information from the iPhone to the Apple Watch. How then, you may ask, can we use this information within our application to provide a useful function? After all, applications should always perform some sort of function to be of any use to the user!

In this section we will use the example of Notation taking the note that is being detected and translating that information into the corresponding image of the note on the Apple Watch's screen.

Importing and Declaring Images

The first thing we should do is import our images into our WatchKit extension's assets folder within our Xcode project. To do this simply select your Images.xcassets folder under your WatchKit Extension folder, click the "+" icon and click "import." Then all you have to do is simply select the images that you are going to use, and click open.

Now that Xcode recognizes our image files, we need to declare them as a global variable (see Listing 5.1). To do this, open up your InterfaceController.m file and inside of your @interface create a UIImage for each image that you are going to use. For instance with Notation we want to create a UIImage for each possible note.

Listing 5.1 Creating UIImages

```
@interface InterfaceController() {
    UIImage *A3StaveCrotchet;
    UIImage *A4StaveCrotchet;
    UIImage *A5StaveCrotchet;

    UIImage *B3StaveCrotchet;
    UIImage *B4StaveCrotchet;
    UIImage *B5StaveCrotchet;

    UIImage *BFlat3StaveCrotchet;
    UIImage *BFlat4StaveCrotchet;
    UIImage *BFlat5StaveCrotchet;

    UIImage *C3StaveCrotchet;
    UIImage *C4StaveCrotchet;
    UIImage *C5StaveCrotchet;

    UIImage *CSharp3StaveCrotchet;
```

```
    UIImage *CSharp4StaveCrotchet;
    UIImage *CSharp5StaveCrotchet;

    UIImage *D3StaveCrotchet;
    UIImage *D4StaveCrotchet;
    UIImage *D5StaveCrotchet;

    UIImage *DSharp3StaveCrotchet;
    UIImage *DSharp4StaveCrotchet;
    UIImage *DSharp5StaveCrotchet;

    UIImage *E3StaveCrotchet;
    UIImage *E4StaveCrotchet;

    UIImage *F3StaveCrotchet;
    UIImage *F4StaveCrotchet;

    UIImage *FSharp3StaveCrotchet;
    UIImage *FSharp4StaveCrotchet;

    UIImage *G2StaveCrotchet;
    UIImage *G3StaveCrotchet;
    UIImage *G4StaveCrotchet;

    UIImage *GSharp2StaveCrotchet;
    UIImage *GSharp3StaveCrotchet;
    UIImage *GSharp4StaveCrotchet;
}
```

Here you can see that we have created several UIImages that are available globally throughout our class, each appropriately named in order for it to be easier for us to recall them later.

Once this is done, the next step is to assign each of these UIImages an image that we imported into our Asset catalog earlier. The best practice for this is to load your images in the class's awakeWithContext object, which is almost identical to the iPhone's viewDidLoad that you are most likely familiar with.

Inside of your awakeWithContext, assign each of the UIImages you declared earlier an Image from your Asset catalog in the following format.

```
UIImage = [UIImage imageNamed:@"IMAGENAME"];
```

For Notation we would write this for every note and awakeWithContext will look something like Listing 5.2.

Listing 5.2. *Applying UIImages to awakeWithContext*

```
- (void)awakeWithContext:(id)context {

    [super awakeWithContext:context];

    A3StaveCrotchet = [UIImage imageNamed:@"A3StaveCrotchet.png"];
```

```objc
    A4StaveCrotchet = [UIImage imageNamed:@"A4StaveCrotchet.png"];
    A5StaveCrotchet = [UIImage imageNamed:@"A5StaveCrotchet.png"];

    B3StaveCrotchet = [UIImage imageNamed:@"B3StaveCrotchet.png"];
    B4StaveCrotchet = [UIImage imageNamed:@"B4StaveCrotchet.png"];
    B5StaveCrotchet = [UIImage imageNamed:@"B5StaveCrotchet.png"];

    BFlat3StaveCrotchet = [UIImage imageNamed:@"BFlat3StaveCrotchet.png"];
    BFlat4StaveCrotchet = [UIImage imageNamed:@"BFlat4StaveCrotchet.png"];
    BFlat5StaveCrotchet = [UIImage imageNamed:@"BFlat5StaveCrotchet.png"];

    C3StaveCrotchet = [UIImage imageNamed:@"C3StaveCrotchet.png"];
    C4StaveCrotchet = [UIImage imageNamed:@"C4StaveCrotchet.png"];
    C5StaveCrotchet = [UIImage imageNamed:@"C5StaveCrotchet.png"];

    CSharp3StaveCrotchet = [UIImage imageNamed:@"CSharp3StaveCrotchet.
png"];
    CSharp4StaveCrotchet = [UIImage imageNamed:@"CSharp4StaveCrotchet.
png"];
    CSharp5StaveCrotchet = [UIImage imageNamed:@"CSharp5StaveCrotchet.
png"];

    D3StaveCrotchet = [UIImage imageNamed:@"D3StaveCrotchet.png"];
    D4StaveCrotchet = [UIImage imageNamed:@"D4StaveCrotchet.png"];
    D5StaveCrotchet = [UIImage imageNamed:@"D5StaveCrotchet.png"];

    DSharp3StaveCrotchet = [UIImage imageNamed:@"DSharp3StaveCrotchet.
png"];
    DSharp4StaveCrotchet = [UIImage imageNamed:@"DSharp4StaveCrotchet.
png"];
    DSharp5StaveCrotchet = [UIImage imageNamed:@"DSharp5StaveCrotchet.
png"];

    E3StaveCrotchet = [UIImage imageNamed:@"E3StaveCrotchet.png"];
    E4StaveCrotchet = [UIImage imageNamed:@"E4StaveCrotchet.png"];

    F3StaveCrotchet = [UIImage imageNamed:@"F3StaveCrotchet.png"];
    F4StaveCrotchet = [UIImage imageNamed:@"F4StaveCrotchet.png"];

    FSharp3StaveCrotchet = [UIImage imageNamed:@"FSharp3StaveCrotchet.
png"];
    FSharp4StaveCrotchet = [UIImage imageNamed:@"FSharp4StaveCrotchet.
png"];

    G2StaveCrotchet = [UIImage imageNamed:@"G2StaveCrotchet.png"];
    G3StaveCrotchet = [UIImage imageNamed:@"G3StaveCrotchet.png"];
    G4StaveCrotchet = [UIImage imageNamed:@"G4StaveCrotchet.png"];

    GSharp2StaveCrotchet = [UIImage imageNamed:@"GSharp2StaveCrotchet.
png"];
    GSharp3StaveCrotchet = [UIImage imageNamed:@"GSharp3StaveCrotchet.
png"];
    GSharp4StaveCrotchet = [UIImage imageNamed:@"GSharp4StaveCrotchet.
png"];
```

```
}
```

So now we have each of the UIImages we created earlier matched up to their appropriate image in our Assets catalog. We use "=" to tell our application that the variable is equal to something and the imageNamed syntax to tell our application that that particular something is an image out of our Asset catalog.

Updating Our Image

Since Apple announced in June that developers could now create Native Apple Watch applications that do not rely on the iPhone, it is possible to do the processing on the Apple Watch itself. There are a number of benefits for doing this, however it is important to remember that the iPhone is a much more powerful device and can therefore process complex things in a much more powerful way. With this in mind it may be recommended to do any large processing tasks on the iPhone.

Now that we have all of our images declared and ready to use we can move on to using them to perform the main function of our application. Inside your InterfaceController.m, create an object called imageUpdate. This will be where the majority of our code handling the changing of our image will be written.

```
-(void)imageUpdate{ }
```

In the last section we explored how to recall information from your App Group. We will start off this function by accessing that data and storing it in our Apple Watch Extension as a float.

```
-(void)imageUpdate{
NSUserDefaults *notationAppGroup = [[NSUserDefaults alloc]
initWithSuiteName: @"group.notation.applewatch"];

float noteValue = [notationAppGroup integerForKey:@"noteValue"];
}
```

Now that we have the note value stored in a float we can use that information to tell our application which image we would like to display in our UIImage. In our example we want to change the image in reference to the different note values we are getting from the iPhone application. Because these values are stored as a float, we can use comparison operators in Objective-C in order to create an IF statement that determines which note is displayed on our Watch screen. Within our function imageUpdate we want to write the following.

```
if(noteValue >= 42.50 && noteValue < 43.50) {
[_watchImage setImage:G2StaveCrotchet];
}
```

Here we can see that in our statement above we are looking at the note value, and if it is between 42.50 and 43.50 then we are setting the WKInterfaceImage (named in our example watchImage) to be our G2StaveCrotchet note icon. You would then repeat this process for each individual note, resulting in a method like this.

```
-(void)imageUpdate{
if(noteValue >= 42.50 && noteValue < 43.50) {
        [_watchImage setImage:G2StaveCrotchet];
    }
else if(noteValue >= 43.50 && noteValue < 44.50) {
        [_watchImage setImage:GSharp2StaveCrotchet]'
    }
else if(noteValue >= 44.50 && noteValue < 45.50) {
        [_watchImage setImage:A3StaveCrotchet];
    }
else if(noteValue >= 45.50 && noteValue < 46.50) {
        [_watchImage setImage:B3StaveCrotchet];
    }
and so on…
}
```

And there we have it! We now have a WatchKit extension that can take a value given to it from its container application and translate that value into visual information. From here we would work out a way of triggering our imageUpdate function, possible methods include:

- Trigger on a button press.

- Using a for(;;) loop to constantly trigger.

- Using a listener delegate to listen for changes to the note.

Summary

Over the course of this chapter we have discussed some of the pitfalls you can encounter when developing an application for the Apple Watch and ways to overcome them. In addition, we have talked about App Groups and how they can be used to share information between the Watch and the iPhone while looking at some of the fundamentals behind Notation. Hopefully you can use this information to start creating a watchOS application of your own and publishing it to the wide and wonderful community of applications on the App Store!

Building the Infinitweet Application

By Ruben Martinez, creator of the Infinitweet Watch app

So far you have learned a lot about the different ways you can go about building Apple Watch apps, and now it is time to actually build a fully-functioning one called Infinitweet. This chapter will introduce you to Infinitweet, a social app for iOS and the Apple Watch. After discussing what the Infinitweet application does and how it is structured, this chapter will then walk you through how to create your first Apple Watch app, a slightly simplified version of the Infinitweet app currently on the App Store.

Though iOS apps can be incredibly complex, Apple Watch apps by comparison are, at this point in time, rather limited in what they can do and how they do it. This chapter will discuss the pros and cons of the limitations of the WatchKit SDK as it pertains to building a real-world app, as well as some creative ways of filling in the gaps ourselves where WatchKit falls short. It will guide you through creating an iOS app and adding an Apple Watch companion app. We will create user interfaces in Storyboard, and learn how to link them back to code. We will discuss the modes of navigating between screens on the Apple Watch, and learn to work with Apple's Social and Accounts frameworks to post to Twitter. Finally, we will learn the magic behind creating Infinitweet. By the end of this chapter, you will have pieced together a fully-functioning, App Store ready app for the Apple Watch.

Introducing Infinitweet

One of the great social media titans to dominate the industry, Twitter has exploded in popularity since it was founded in 2006. As an active Twitter user since joining in 2011, I had been closely watching a trend in recent months towards sharing screenshots of text on the social media website. Through this method, users of Twitter were able to share more content on Twitter, bypassing the infamous 140 character limit, created for a time when tweets were primarily sent through SMS. Though this method was functional, it was often inelegant, and resulted in shots of text that were either cropped due to Twitter's own image guidelines, or too small to comfortably read.

In January 2015, I set off to work on Infinitweet. Infinitweet is a Twitter app that can take text, along with formatting, such as fonts and colors, and convert it into an image. It leverages many of iOS's built-in frameworks to draw text within a container and allows the user to share it to Twitter. This way, tweets can be as long as the user wants them to be without getting in the way of character limits! Best of all, Infinitweet is smart enough to resize the image to fit perfectly within the bounds of Twitter's image previews, meaning there is no cropped text. As an example of an Infinitweet, see Figure 6.1.

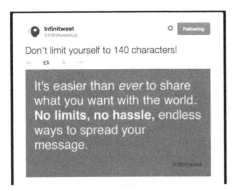

Figure 6.1. An Infinitweet as seen on Twitter

Though the original target audience was people who tend to be a bit long-winded in tweets, or just people who needed to share longer-than-usual tweets, Infinitweet for the Apple Watch took on a whole new role. The Watch app is much simpler and more streamlined than the phone app. To create an Infinitweet, the user simply taps the new tweet icon, speaks their tweet, approves the previewed image, and voila! Whereas the iPhone app's aim is to maximize customizability of a tweet of any length, the Watch app uses default settings from the parent iOS app to maximize simplicity and prevent the user from having to worry about going over any character limits. The last thing a user wants to be thinking about while they tweet from their wrist is whether they are going over 140 characters.

After being endorsed by the notorious "tweet-storming" venture capitalist Marc Andreesen on Twitter, Infinitweet made it to #6 on ProductHunt when it launched its most recent iteration in April, and it has since been downloaded thousands of times across iOS, Android, and Chrome. Around the same time as Infinitweet launched, similar apps like OneShot popped up as well, and the popular blogging site, Medium, built in a web tool that lets users highlight text to share it as an image to Twitter.

Environment-Driven Feature Sets

Apple Watch apps are quite often much more limited than iOS apps, both due to constraints set by Apple, as well as limitations inherent to the device itself. The two most important of these limitations are the smaller screen real-estate and the presumably shorter user attention span. However, rather than being a burden, these limitations both create the opportunity for simplification of advanced features and streamlining, and also make things easier for new developers to pick up.

Infinitweet for iOS

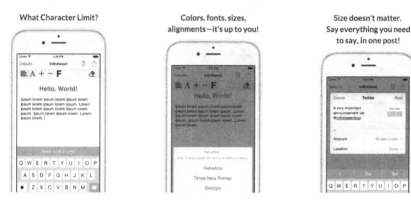

Figure 6.2. A promotional image for Infinitweet

As evidenced by Figure 6.2, a priority from day one for the Infinitweet app for iOS was keeping the user interface as simple and uncluttered as possible. First and foremost, the goal was to eliminate any and all friction between the user's thoughts and their ability to send a tweet of any length. Because this is an app for sharing potentially sizeable chunks of text, it made sense to make the primary focus of this app an empty UITextView, a blank canvas for the user to craft their tweet on.

When the user opens the app, the UITextView is made the first responder; this means that they can immediately use the keyboard to enter in any text they want to share. They can then use the buttons in the UIToolbar above the UITextView to change things like font, font color, background, alignments, bold, italics, and underlining in any piece of text by highlighting it. The app automatically backs up any changes locally until the user is ready to share their creation, so in the event of an app crash or other error, whatever the text or formatting is on screen is backed up. When the user is ready to send their Infinitweet off to Twitter, they can press the share button in the UINavigationBar.

This fires off the Infinitweet algorithm, which converts the text into an image. We will discuss how this algorithm works in further detail in a later section. Once the Infinitweet we created is ready, the user is presented with a Share Sheet, which lets them choose what to do with the final image. If there are certain fonts or styles they like to use all the time, there is an option to set these as Defaults. As we will see in a moment, these options are able to propagate themselves to the Apple Watch.

Infinitweet for Apple Watch

Figure 6.3. *Infinitweet for Apple Watch*

When designing for the Watch, less is more. For centuries, watchmakers have referred to additional features on a watch, like a chronograph or different time zone feature as "complications." It is good to adopt a similar philosophy when developing for Apple Watch because more complications are more of a burden for the user to work through. The Infinitweet Apple Watch app, then, excludes many of the complications central to the phone app.

The Watch app does not let the user change fonts, colors, styling, layouts, etc. of the Infinitweet that they create. Instead, these are preset according to the Defaults they have set in the parent iOS app. To do this, Infinitweet takes advantage of a feature called App Groups, which let the developer, among other things, share data using NSUserDefaults between an iOS app, an App Extension, and/or an Apple Watch app. So, because we know what we want the Infinitweet to look like ahead of time, there is no need for context menus, toolbars, or overly-complex settings; we just take the input, run the Infinitweet algorithm, and present the Infinitweet image to the user for sharing.

More generally, when building apps for Apple Watch, the aim should be to simplify the interface for the user as much as possible without losing core functionality. One of the aims I had while building the Infinitweet app for the Apple Watch was to keep the number of taps required as low as possible in order to make sending an Infinitweet as simple and easy as possible, even if that meant cutting super-user features. If the user had to press through ten different screens to do what they came to the app to do, they will reach for their phone and won't bother opening the Watch app the next time they need to use your service.

In addition to the above user experience constraints, the Apple Watch developer needs to keep in mind the user interface. Here is another area where we strive for clarity and simplicity, perhaps even more so than on the phone. On the Apple Watch's 38mm or 42mm display, it is paramount that text and buttons be as large as possible in order to make using your app a painless experience for the user. If you make your touch targets too small, it could create a frustrating experience for the user. Fortunately, Apple makes this part easy for us by creating well-sized default button sizes. Though we can change the size of these some, it is often better to trust Apple's defaults.

The Infinitweet Watch app, then, keeps things simple in terms of the options presented, and keeps them clear and readable. Additionally, as seen in Figure 6.3, it is limited to three primary screens: the initial home screen, the input screen where we take text input, and the preview screen where we see the resulting Infinitweet and have the option to share it. However, because in WatchOS there is no built-in way to do social media sharing, unlike with Share Sheets on iOS, the developer is tasked with leveraging a slightly more low-level approach to sharing to social media sites like Twitter. Using the Social framework and Accounts framework, we have to first get permissions from the user on their iOS device to use their social media account (only once per user), present the user with options to share from any of their linked Twitter accounts, and share from the selected account.

So Where Does the Magic Happen?

Part of the beauty of Infinitweet is that it all happens locally on the phone—not remotely on a server. While there is no network access involved in creating the Infinitweet, we of course need network access to share to Twitter, Facebook, or anywhere else online. However, the creation of the Infinitweet happens on the iOS device regardless of where the Infinitweet gets its input. In other words, the creation and processing of Infinitweet happens on the iPhone, even with the Apple Watch app. The Apple Watch "app" is purely front-end, and handles basic display logic; any heavy processing happens on the WatchKit Extension, and the division is clean enough that the developer does not usually have to think about it while making the app. While native apps that run exclusively on the Watch are coming in watchOS 2 , the Infinitweet algorithm requires heavy enough processing that it will always be beneficial to have it run on the beefier phone processor.

Building Infinitweet

So let's get started building our Apple Watch app, Infinitweet. This guide will walk through creating an iOS app in Xcode, creating an Apple Watch app, and then incrementally adding features to the Watch app. Ensure you have the latest Xcode installed on your Mac before you begin.

Getting Started

Open Xcode and create a new Project (File ➤ New ➤ Project). Since we are going to keep the iOS portion of the application as simple as possible in order to focus on the Apple Watch app, ensure the Single View Application option is selected, as shown in Figure 6.4, and press the Next button to continue.

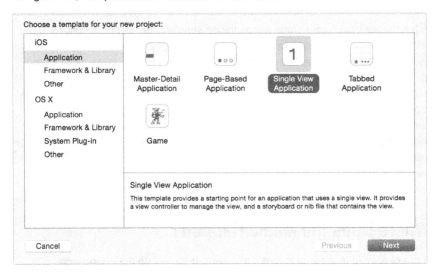

Figure 6.4. Creating a new application

Once on the next screen, you can fill out the necessary fields and name the application as you like. For our purposes, we will call the application Infinitweet. Ensure that Swift is selected for the language and iPhone for devices because we will not bother making this a universal application. When you are ready, the screen should look like Figure 6.5. Press Next, select a place to store your project, and continue on to the main development environment.

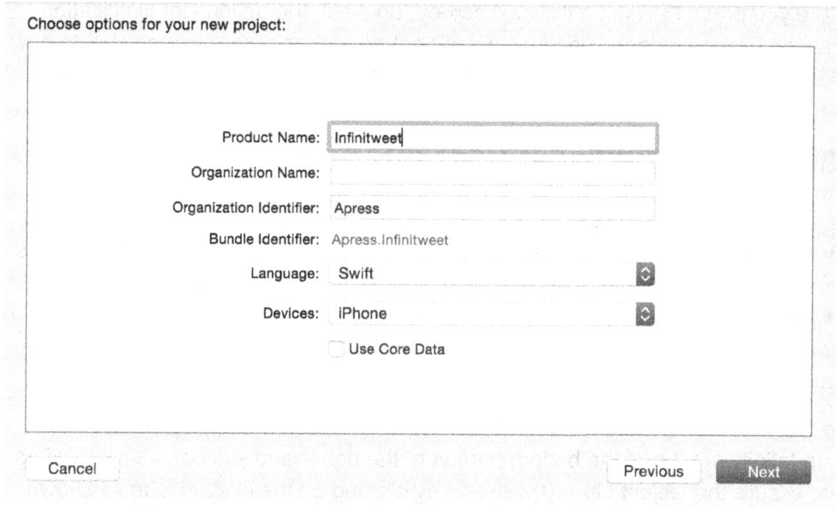

Choose options for your new project:

Product Name: | Infinitweet

Organization Name:

Organization Identifier: | Apress

Bundle Identifier: Apress.Infinitweet

Language: Swift

Devices: iPhone

☐ Use Core Data

Cancel   Previous   Next

Figure 6.5. Creating a new application (continued)

Congratulations, we have an iOS app! Our next step is to create a companion Apple Watch app. Go to File ➤ New ➤ Target. Select Apple Watch from the sidebar and ensure WatchKit App is selected before pressing Next.

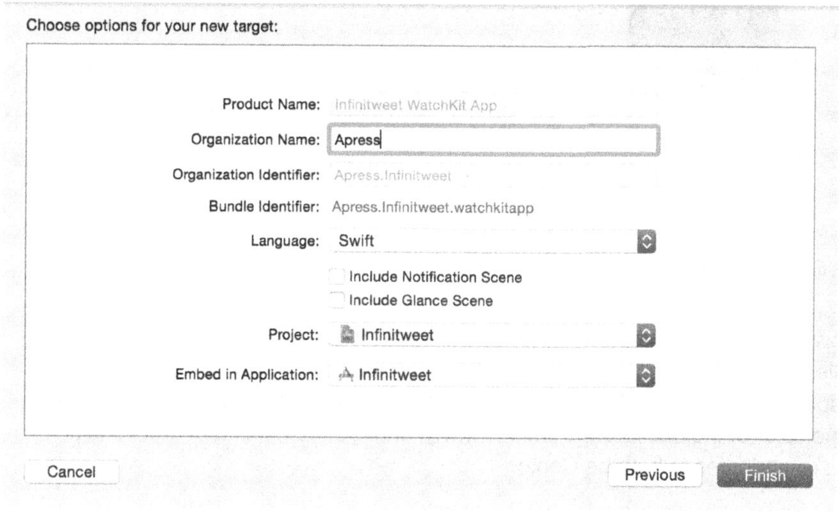

Choose options for your new target:

Product Name: | Infinitweet WatchKit App

Organization Name: | Apress

Organization Identifier: Apress.Infinitweet

Bundle Identifier: Apress.Infinitweet.watchkitapp

Language: Swift

☐ Include Notification Scene
☐ Include Glance Scene

Project: Infinitweet

Embed in Application: Infinitweet

Cancel   Previous   Finish

Figure 6.6. Adding a WatchKit app to our application

Before you press `Finish` on the next screen, uncheck the options for Notification screens and Glance screens because we will not need those. Your screen should now look like Figure 6.6. We're now ready to get started building our Apple Watch app!

Creating the Infinitweet User Interface

As discussed earlier, Infinitweet for the Apple Watch has a very simple user interface. Now we can begin to recreate it! Within the left-hand sidebar in Xcode, also known as the Navigator, and under the "Infinitweet Watchkit App" folder, click on the file named `Interface.storyboard`. Here we will recreate the user interface that we see above in Figure 6.3. The three primary stages of the app will here translate to our first three Interface Controllers.

The first is the simplest. All we have is a centered button prompting the user to begin an Infinitweet. From the bottom portion of the right-hand sidebar, also known as Utilities, ensure the Object Library is shown by clicking on the circular icon as shown in Figure 6-7. Then, click and drag a `Button` from the Object Library into the empty `Interface Controller` visible in the main window.

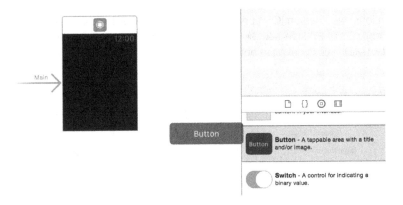

Figure 6.7. Dragging a Button from the Object Library

Now, the Attributes inspector within the top part of Utilities should automatically be selected, but if not, click it. Ensuring the `Button` is selected in the Storyboard workspace, change the Title attribute to "Infinitweet." Make the color of the text black, and the color of the background white. Finally, change the horizontal and vertical `Position` attributes to both be Center.

Note Unlike in iOS apps, WatchKit apps are more restrictive as to where you can place things within a controller. Though you can fix the widths of UI elements, all positioning is relative. After this step, your Attributes should look like those in Figure 6.8.

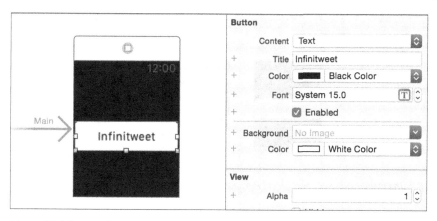

Figure 6.8. Infinitweet Button attributes

The second of Infinitweet's Interface Controllers is the voice input controller, and we will be creating it later in this tutorial in code, so that brings us to the last of the primary controllers, the Infinitweet preview controller. This Interface Controller shows the user a preview of the Infinitweet we generated before it is posted to Twitter.

Drag another Interface Controller from the Object Library to the Storyboard area. Go to the Attributes Inspector and set the Identifier attribute to PreviewController. This will let us show this controller from the code later on. As you can see in Figure 6.3, this controller has two parts: a Button in the lower half, and an Image in the top half.

First, drag an Image into the PreviewController. Center it vertically and horizontally like we did with the Infinitweet Button earlier, by changing the horizontal and vertical Position attributes to Center.

Next, drag a Button into the PreviewController. By default, the button and anything else you drag will have a position of top-left, so it will appear above the Image initially. To position it where we want it, set the vertical Position attribute to bottom, and the horizontal to center for good measure. Change the Title attribute to "Share," and set the text color to black and background to white so it is consistent with our Infinitweet Button from the first controller.

After this controller, your workspace should look like Figure 6.9. We're not done with Interface Controllers just yet, but for now let's get this interface to talk with our code.

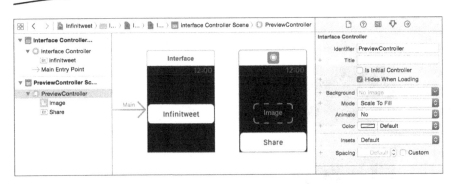

Figure 6.9. The main Interface Controller and PreviewController

Communicating Between Storyboard and Code

Now for the fun part: getting the interface we just created to communicate with the code so that it can actually work. Under Navigator, go to the folder "Infinitweet WatchKit Extension" and click on the file `InterfaceController.swift`. This `InterfaceController` class, a subclass of `WKInterfaceController`, will control the behavior of the `Interface Controller` view we made a few moments ago.

To begin, we need to create a reference to the Infinitweet button we added to this `Interface Controller` in Storyboard. We do this using an `IBOutlet`, which connects a user interface element in Storyboard with a particular class. Their companions, `IBActions`, connect user interface actions with methods in a class. We will create some of these in just a moment as well.

For now, double-click on the `Interface.Storyboard` file in Navigator to open the file in a new window. You should now have both the Storyboard visible in one window, and the `InterfaceController.swift` file visible in another. While pressing and holding the control button, click and drag from the Infinitweet button to the top of the `InterfaceController` class file; position your mouse within the class, but outside of the methods. You should see a blue line following your mouse. Once you release, you will have the option to add in `IBOutlet`, as in Figure 6.10. Name this button `tweetButton`, and press Connect. This should give you a line like the following:

```
@IBOutlet weak var tweetButton: WKInterfaceButton!
```

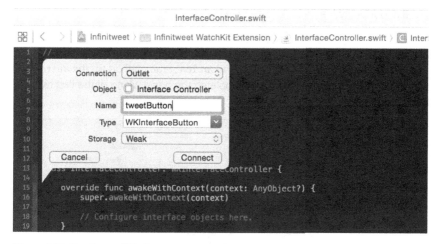

Figure 6.10. *Creating an IBOutlet*

This IBOutlet will allow us to reference and manipulate the Infinitweet button the user sees on screen. In order to get the button to execute an action when tapped, however, we need to create an IBAction. Repeat the same series of steps we used to create an IBOutlet, except this time, change the Connection option as visible in Figure 6.10 from Outlet to Action. We can call this action captureTweet. The method this creates will control what the button does when pressed by the user. Before we implement the details of this behavior, however, we should wire up the PreviewController we created earlier.

While the Interface Controller's class file was given to us, we must create a new WKInterfaceController subclass for our PreviewController. First, ensure the Infinitweet WatchKit Extension folder is selected, so that the file we create ends up within the Extension. Go to File ➤ New ➤ File. Select the Source option on the left sidebar, and choose Cocoa Touch Class within the window before clicking the Next button. Make the file a subclass of WKInterfaceController, name it PreviewController, and then click Next. Choose a location to save the file (the default is usually fine) and then finish. We now have our new class skeleton in a file, PreviewController.swift.

Our next step is to tell the PreviewController we created in Storyboard earlier that it is of the same class PreviewController that we just created. To do this, navigate to the Interface.Storyboard file and click on the outer frame of the PreviewController so that it is selected. This should feature a blue outline when it is selected. Then, in the Utilities sidebar, click on the Identity Inspector icon. Here we can set a custom class; in our case, we wish to set the Class attribute to PreviewController. The

Storyboard and Identity Inspector should now look like Figure 6.11.

Our `PreviewController` in Storyboard features an `Image` and a `Button`. Following the steps we used to create an `IBOutlet` for the last button, create an `IBOutlet` for the `Image`, which we will call `imageDisplay`, and an `IBAction` method for the `Button`, which we will simply call `share`. We have completed the basic wiring of the first two controllers!

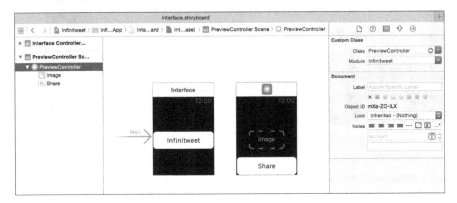

Figure 6.11. Setting a Custom Class for an Interface Controller

Capturing User Voice Input

As you will recall, the missing controller we did not create was for capturing voice input from the user and needed to be made in code. We will do this from the `InterfaceController`, specifically in the `captureTweet` method. To prompt the user for voice input, we use the built-in `TextInputController`, which we can activate using the function: `presentTextInputControllerWithSuggestions(suggestions: [AnyObject]?, allowedInputMode inputMode: WKTextInputMode, completion: ([AnyObject]!) -> Void)`. This function lets us ask the user for input and provide the user with suggestions. Now, populate the `captureTweet` method as follows:

```
@IBAction func captureTweet() {
        self.presentTextInputControllerWithSuggestions(["Infinitweeting via
Apple Watch!"], allowedInputMode: WKTextInputMode.Plain) { (results) ->
Void in
                // Ensure we received user input
                if results != nil && results.count > 0 {
                    let text = results.first as! String //the user input as
text

                    // TODO: create infinitweet here

                    // We don't need this controller anymore
                    self.dismissTextInputController()
```

```
            // TODO: navigate to next controller
        }
    }
}
```

Let's break down what this brief chunk of code does. First, we present the `TextInputController` with the suggestion "Infinitweeting via Apple Watch!" and only allow plain text to be input using the option `WKTextInputMode.Plain`. We could, alternatively, have allowed for things like Apple Watch's animated emoji, but that is not a desirable input form in our case. Within the closure we pass as an argument, we first ensure that we got some sort of input from the user, and if we did, we store that input within the constant `text`. After that, we need to turn the input to an Infinitweet, which we will do later, dismiss the `TextInputController`, which takes us back to the home screen, and finally, navigate to the next controller, which we will discuss in the next section.

Navigating Between WKInterfaceControllers

Navigation in the Apple Watch user interface often takes one of two forms: presenting and dismissing, or pushing and popping. We will use mostly pushing and popping, which is the primary mode of hierarchical navigation. Presenting and dismissing is used primarily for interstitial controllers, like the `TextInputController` we just used.

Now that we have each of our `Interface Controllers` set up, the next step is to connect them to each other. The first connections were already put in place above: tapping the Infinitweet button presents the `TextInputController`, and successfully capturing voice input dismisses it. The next step is pushing our `PreviewController` onto the stack and passing it the Infinitweet we generate.

To begin, let's replace the TODO's we left above with actual code. In place of the line:

```
// TODO: create infinitweet here
```

Insert the following lines:

```
// TODO: actually create infinitweet here
let infinitweet = nil
```

This will give us an error at first, but it's okay. This is just so we can use the Infinitweet variable in the next TODO we replace. We will do the actual work of creating an Infinitweet a bit later, in the Infinitweet Algorithm section. For now, let's replace our next to do. Replace the line:

```
// TODO: navigate to next controller
```

with the working lines:

```
// Passes Infinitweet to PreviewController and presents it
self.pushControllerWithName("PreviewController", context: ["infinitweet":
infinitweet.image])
```

This line pushes the next controller, the `PreviewController`, onto the user interface stack, and passes it the dictionary containing the Infinitweet we have created, so that it can display it to the user for approval.

Now that the initial `InterfaceController`'s navigation is set up, let's do the same for the `PreviewController`. First, we should store the Infinitweet we just passed the `PreviewController`. We need to create a global variable to store the Infinitweet image so that we can use it in different parts of our code. At the top of the class, after our `IBOutle imageDisplay`, add the following line:

```
var imageToShare : UIImage?
```

> **Note** It is important to remember that `imageToShare` contains the actual `UIImage` we will be displaying and sharing, whereas the `IBOutlet` we created earlier is a reference to the user interface element we created in Storyboard that will merely display the `UIImage`.

The `awakeWithContext` method that was created automatically for you when you created the `PreviewController` class contains a local copy of the context that we passed the `PreviewController` from `InterfaceController`. Extract the Infinitweet from that dictionary and store the image by adding the following lines at the end of the `awakeWithContext` method:

```
if context != nil && context!.objectForKey("image") != nil {
    self.imageToShare = (context!.objectForKey("image") as? UIImage)
    self.imageDisplay.setImage(self.imageToShare)
}
```

This checks to make sure we were passed a context with an image, and if so, stores it and adds it to the `imageDisplay`, making it visible to the user.

Now that we have the transition to the `PreviewController` handled, we need to handle the transition away from it. Within the `share` method, which we will fill in more in the next section, simply add the following line:

```
self.popToRootController()
```

This line makes it so that once the `PreviewController` is shown, pressing the share button will bring us back to the `InterfaceController` we pushed the `PreviewController` from, though at this point, nothing is actually shared. We will handle that in the next section. This completes the basic navigation between controllers in the Infinitweet app!

Working with Social and Account Frameworks

The next step is where we get a bit more code intensive: working with the Social and Account frameworks to post to the user's Twitter account. Unlike on the iPhone or iPad, where we have Share Sheets to allow the user to select the account that they want to share things from, on the Apple Watch we have to take matters into our own hands. The key ingredients here are the Social and Account frameworks, which allow us access to the user's synced social media accounts (e.g. Facebook,

Twitter, etc.) and let us share things through those channels without the need for user authentication on every share and without having to store any credentials ourselves.

To begin using the Social and Account frameworks, we must first import them into code; in our case, we want the following two lines at the very top of `PreviewController.swift`, the file controlling the view in which the user approves the Infinitweet for sharing:

```
import Social
import Accounts
```

Now that we can access the methods within these frameworks, let's replace our current `share` method with a little more logic:

```
@IBAction func share() {
        // Load Synced Account Database
        let accountStore = ACAccountStore()

        // Specify Type of Account we want to use
        let accountType = accountStore.
accountTypeWithAccountTypeIdentifier(ACAccountTypeIdentifierTwitter)

        // TODO: Determine whether we already have access to the user's
Twitter account
        // Prompt user for permission to use their Twitter account
        accountStore.requestAccessToAccountsWithType(accountType, options:
nil) {
            granted, error in

            if granted {
                let twitterAccounts = accountStore.accountsWithAccountType(
accountType)

                if twitterAccounts.count == 0 {
                    // TODO: No Twitter accounts synced by user
                }
                else if twitterAccounts.count > 1 {
                    // TODO: User has more than one Twitter account
                }
                else {
                    // TODO: User has one Twitter account, post to that one
                }
            }
            else {
                // TODO: Access not granted by user
            }
        }
    }
```

That's a lot to take in at first, but it's actually all fairly straight forward. The first thing we do is create an `ACAccountStore` object, which allows us to access any accounts stored on the user's iOS device. In the next line, we define a constant `accountType`, which stores the account type that matches the identifier (in this case, the Twitter identifier, `ACAccountTypeIdentifierTwitter`). We use this in the following line to request access to any accounts that have this type. This prompts the user to give us access to their account, but unfortunately, it does so on the iOS device, not the watch. We will handle that later.

In the following if...else, we deal with whether or not the user gives us access to their account. If the user does give us access, we store an array of all their Twitter accounts, and have to deal with a few edge-cases: namely, what to do when a user gives us access but doesn't have any accounts, or has more than one account. Additionally, we must define the normal behavior when a user only has one account.

Let's start by defining the normal behavior. Outside of the share function entirely, create a new method called `postImageToAccount(account : ACAccount)`. This method will take care of posting the image we stored in `imageToShare` earlier. Fill out the method as follows:

```
func postImageToAccount(account : ACAccount) {
    if let image = self.imageToShare {
        // URL for posting an image, according to Twitter API
        let requestURL = NSURL(string: "https://api.twitter.com/1.1/
statuses/update_with_media.json")

        // Prepare image posting request
        var postRequest = SLRequest(forServiceType: SLServiceTypeTwitter,
requestMethod: SLRequestMethod.POST, URL: requestURL, parameters: nil)
        postRequest.addMultipartData(UIImageJPEGRepresentation(image 1.0),
withName: "media[]", type: "multipart/form-data", filename: nil)
        postRequest.addMultipartData("".dataUsingEncoding(NSUTF8StringEnco
ding, allowLossyConversion: false), withName: "status", type: "multipart/
form-data", filename: nil)
        postRequest.account = account

        postRequest.performRequestWithHandler({ (responseData, urlResponse,
error) -> Void in
            if error == nil {
                // TODO: We succeeded!
            } else {
                // TODO: We ran into an error
            }
        })
    }
}
```

Let's break this up the same way we broke up the `share` method. The first thing we do in `postImageToAccount` is check whether the image we will be posting actually exists. It should, as we filled stored it in the `awakeWithContext` method earlier, but better safe than sorry. If it does, we store it in the constant `image` and proceed.

Next, we define `requestURL`, the URL we will be making the request to post the image to as per the Twitter API. This URL will vary depending on the type of request you want to make, the API version you are using, and the service you are requesting to. In our case, this is the proper URL for posting an image to Twitter as of API version 1.1. In the following few lines, we define an `SLRequest` object, which allows us to make an HTTP request. In the initialization of the `SLRequest`, we specify that we want to make a POST request to the Twitter service at `requestURL`.

The `addMultiPartData` calls allow us to specify parameters we want for the request; the Twitter API tells us posts to the `requestURL` require the parameters "media[]" and "status," the former containing the image we want to post and the latter containing any text accompanying the image. In order to attach the image, we have to convert it to a JPEG, so we use the function UIImageJPEGRepresentation, which takes a UIImage and a value from 0.0 to 1.0 that gives the compression quality of the resulting JPEG. We then associate this with the "media[]" parameter and add it to the request. For the "status" parameter, we similarly wrap a string in UTF8 encoding and attach it to the request. In this example, it is left blank, though it could contain any text you wish to attach to the Infinitweet image such as, "Posted via Infinitweet!"

The next line simply tells the SLRequest to use the ACAccount we were passed to authenticate. In that simple line, we avoid having to deal with usernames or passwords because Apple does all the hard work for us without us ever having to handle sensitive information.

Finally, the performRequestWithHandler call tells the request to execute and provides a closure for handling the response. We will handle this at a later point, but for now we simply divide it into an if...else of whether or not we have an error.

To recap this section, we have now implemented the majority of the logic for sharing an Infinitweet to Twitter. We can now, for a given UIImage and ACAccount, post the image to Twitter. To tie it all together, however, we need one more line. Within the share method, replace the line:

```
// TODO: User has one Twitter account, post to that one
```

with the working call to the method we just created:

```
self.postImageToAccount(twitterAccounts.first as! ACAccount)
```

In the next section, we will add code that handles one of our edge cases: users with more than one Twitter account.

Prompting the User With Options

Many users of Twitter, including myself, tend to have multiple Twitter accounts synced to their phone. How do we know which one the user wants to post to? This is a non-issue on the iPhone or iPad, where we simply summon a ShareSheet to take care of the hard work. Still, some apps will use the first Twitter account synced to the phone, a crude solution that works, but which doesn't let the user decide. We will approach this issue by creating an entirely new Interface Controller that will ask the user which account they want to share from using a new UI tool, WKInterfaceTables.

Navigate to the Interface.Storyboard file. From the Object Library, drag in a brand new Interface Controller. In the Attributes Inspector, set the Identifier of this controller to "AccountsController" so that we can refer to it from the code later. Drag into the AccountsController a Label and set the Position attributes in the Attributes Inspector to horizontal Center, vertical Top. Change the Text Alignment to Centered and set the label Text to "Select a Twitter Account." Unfortunately, this will cut off the text because it does not all fit on one line. To fix this, change the Lines attribute value to 0; this will tell the Label to use as many lines as it needs to fit the text.

Next, add in a Table. We will use this to display the user's Twitter accounts as options. In the Attributes Inspector, set the Position to horizontal Center, vertical Bottom. Into the Table, drag in a Label. This will automatically create a Table Row Controller. Click on it and set the Identifier attribute to "AccountRow." That will allow us to reference it as a row prototype from the code. Next, click on the Group nested in the AccountRow controller and set the Background Color to White; then, click on the Label we just dragged in, set the Text Color to Black, and change the vertical Position attribute to Center. When finished, your AccountsController should look like Figure 6.12. We've completed the Storyboard portion of the Interface Controller and can transition back to the code!

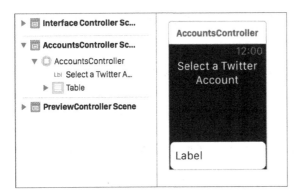

Figure 6.12. *Completed AccountsController*

Now, let's create a new WKInterfaceController subclass using the same method we used for the PreviewController. Call this one AccountsController. This class will control the behavior of the Table we created earlier, presenting the user with the option to post from any of their accounts, and using the selected account to post our Infinitweet. Before we jump into the code, we need to link the AccountsController we created in Storyboard with the new AccountsController class. In the right sidebar, under the Identity Inspector for our AccountsController, set the Class to AccountsController. Now, open up the recently created AccountsController.swift file in a new window. Like we did earlier, hold down the control key and drag from the Table (ensure the Table is selected, not the group or the label) we created in Storyboard into the Swift file to create an IBOutlet of type WKInterfaceTable which we will call accountsTable.

The accountsTable will have multiple rows, each of which will display a different account the user has synced to their device. In order to do this, we must additionally create a new NSObject subclass the same way we just created a WKInterfaceController subclass, and call this class AccountRow. Back in Storyboard, we must change the Class of the Table Row Controller to AccountRow. Now, opening the Storyboard in a new window, hold the control key and drag from the Label we added earlier into the AccountRow class to create an IBOutlet for the WKInterfaceLabel we will simply call name. Now each instance of AccountRow has a name attribute that we can modify to be the name of the account. Before this will work, we must add the statement import WatchKit to the top of the class, so the AccountRow class knows what a WKInterfaceLabel is. With this, we can begin filling in our code.

Navigate to the PreviewController class file. Remove the line:

```
// TODO: User has more than one Twitter account
```

We can instead handle the edge case by prompting the user to select a Twitter account, which we will do in the AccountsController. Add the line:

```
self.presentControllerWithName("AccountsController", context: ["accounts":
twitterAccounts])
```

This will present our AccountsController to the user, passing it an array with all of the Twitter accounts the user has synced to the device. Back in the AccountsController file, we must import the Accounts framework into the AccountsController by adding the statement import Accounts to the top of the file. Then, declare an array to store the passed Twitter accounts by adding the following line after the accountsTable IBOutlet declaration:

```
var accounts : [ACAccount]?
```

Then, within the awakeWithContext method, add the following lines:

```
if context != nil {
    // Store the list of accounts
    self.accounts = context!.objectForKey("accounts") as? [ACAccount]

    if self.accounts != nil {
        // Set number of rows to number of Accounts
        self.accountsTable.setNumberOfRows(self.accounts!.count,
withRowType: "AccountRow")
        //Populate rows with Account usernames
        for var i = 0; i < self.accountsTable.numberOfRows; i++ {
            var row = self.accountsTable.rowControllerAtIndex(i) as!
AccountRow
            row.name.setText("@\(self.accounts![i].username)")
        }
    }
}
```

This first stores the list of accounts passed to the AccountsController for later use. Then, checking that the list of accounts exists, it populates the Table by setting the number of rows in the table to the number of accounts in our list. Finally, it sets the name attribute of each row in the table to correspond to the username associated with each account.

Now that we've shown the user a list of the accounts they have synced to their device, we must define the behavior that happens when one of these rows is selected. Add in the following method to the AccountsController class:

```
override func table(table: WKInterfaceTable, didSelectRowAtIndex rowIndex:
Int) {
    // TODO: Post Infinitweet to selected account
```

```
}
```

This method, which overrides the default method for describing what happens on row selection, is the final piece of the WKInterfaceTable puzzle. It will post the Infinitweet image that we created earlier to the Twitter account corresponding to the selected row. In order to do this, however, we need to define a delegate protocol that will allow us to call the postImageToAccount method we defined earlier.

At the end of the file, after the final close bracket, paste in the following code:

```
protocol AccountSelectionDelegate {
    func postImageToAccount(account : ACAccount)
}
```

This definition allows us to call the method postImageToAccount on any class that implements the AccountSelectionDelegate protocol. In order to do that, we must give our AccountsController class access to this delegate class. But first thing's first: navigate to the PreviewController and change the class definition to read:

```
class PreviewController: WKInterfaceController, AccountSelectionDelegate
```

We already have the only delegate method, postImageToAccount, defined, so we have already adhered to the protocol. Now, we need to pass our PreviewController to our AccountsController so that it can set it as its delegate. Modify the line within the share method that reads:

```
self.presentControllerWithName("AccountsController", context: ["accounts":
twitterAccounts])
```

to instead read:

```
self.presentControllerWithName("AccountsController", context: ["accounts":
twitterAccounts, "delegate" : self])
```

This will pass the PreviewController to the AccountsController as part of the context dictionary we are already using to pass the array of Twitter accounts. Now, at the top of the AccountsController class, add in the line:

```
var delegate : AccountSelectionDelegate?
```

This will allow us to store the delegate as a global variable. In the awakeWithContext method, below the initialization of self.accounts, add in the line:

```
self.delegate = (context!.objectForKey("delegate") as! PreviewController)
```

This will store the PreviewController we passed as a global delegate to the AccountsController class. Finally, within the tableDidSelectRowAtIndex, replace the //TODO comment with the following lines:

```
delegate?.postImageToAccount(self.accounts![rowIndex])
self.dismissController()
```

This will call the postImageToAccount method of the PreviewController class and pass it the account at the selected index, taking care of our edge case. It will then dismiss the AccountsController, bringing focus back to our PreviewController. Our app now handles users with multiple Twitter accounts!

The Infinitweet Algorithm

Believe it or not, our Infinitweet app for Apple Watch is almost complete! However, we are still missing a few crucial parts, one of which is actually generating Infinitweets. Let's create a new class called `Infinitweet`. Go to File ➤ New ➤ File. Select Swift File, and press Next. Name the file Infinitweet.Swift and continue. Replace any code in the Swift file with the following:

```
import Foundation
import UIKit

class Infinitweet {
    // Will store Infinitweet image after initialization
    var image : UIImage

    // TODO: Define default Infinitweet Properties

    init(text : String) {
        let ratio = 2  as CGFloat // Twitter images in stream appear in 2:1
aspect ratio
        let delta = 10 as CGFloat // Amount to adjust image width by per
cycle
        let maxCycles = 1000     // After this many cycles, give up

        // TODO: Set text properties

        // TODO: Set initial image attempt properties

        // TODO: Approximate Infinitweet image ratio

        // TODO: Get final Infinitweet size

        // TODO: Generate image
    }

    // Tells us which way the Infinitweet was adjusted
    enum InfinitweetDelta {
        case Positive, Negative
    }
}
```

This basic template will allow us to get started building up our Infinitweet algorithm. Let's walk through what we want the Infinitweet algorithm to do. In place of the line:

```
// TODO: Define default Infinitweet Properties
```

Add the code:

```
// Default Infinitweet Properties
let defaultFont       = UIFont.systemFontOfSize(16)
let defaultColor      = UIColor.blackColor()
let defaultBackground = UIColor.whiteColor()
let defaultPadding    = 20.0 as CGFloat
```

This will define all of the properties the Infinitweet image will have. In a more complete version of the Infinitweet app, we could make these properties user adjustable, but for now we will hard code them.

At the top of the class we have an `image` property, which will store the Infinitweet image we will create. The custom initializer we defined takes a string, `text`, and will generate the image to be stored.

One of the key features of Infinitweet is its ability to generate text images that fit within Twitter's image preview windows. In order to do this, it has to make the images fit a 2 by 1 width to height aspect ratio. Though iOS has built-in tools for converting text to images, there is no way to predefine an aspect ratio. We can, however, set a fixed width and test the resulting height to see if it meets our desired aspect ratio. We can then adjust this width by a certain delta until we have the aspect ratio we want. Though there are faster ways to reach this ratio, for this example we will simply adjust the width incrementally. In place of our next TODO, add the following code:

```
// Set text properties
let options = unsafeBitCast(NSStringDrawingOptions.UsesLineFragmentOrigin.
rawValue | NSStringDrawingOptions.UsesFontLeading.rawValue,
NSStringDrawingOptions.self)
let textAttributes = [NSFontAttributeName: defaultFont,
NSForegroundColorAttributeName: defaultColor]
```

The first line is a set of options that will define how the text will draw onto the image. The second line describes what the text will look like by giving it a font and color. Now, replace the next TODO with the following lines:

```
// Set initial image attempt properties
var currentWidth = 200 as CGFloat
var imageSize = (text as NSString).boundingRectWithSize(CGSizeMake(currentW
idth, CGFloat.max), options: options, attributes: textAttributes, context:
nil)

var currentHeight = imageSize.height
var lastRatio = currentWidth/currentHeight
var lastDelta = InfinitweetDelta.Positive
```

The first statement stores the initial test width into a variable called `currentWidth`. The second line calculates a size for the rectangle encompassing the given text constrained to that width. It also takes into account the options and attributes we defined above. Next, we store the calculated height of the rectangle into a variable, `currentHeight`, and store the width to height ratio into a variable `lastRatio`. Finally, the variable `lastDelta` will tell us whether we just increased the width or decreased it, so we can backtrack if necessary. We set it to positive, or increased, as default.

The next step is the bulk of the algorithm: approximating a 2 by 1 aspect ratio in a loop. In place of the line:

```
// TODO: Approximate Infinitweet image ratio
```

add the following code:

```
var cycleCount = 0
while cycleCount++ < maxCycles {
    if lastRatio >= ratio {
        currentWidth -= delta
        lastDelta = InfinitweetDelta.Negative
    } else {
        currentWidth += delta
        lastDelta = InfinitweetDelta.Positive
    }

    // Recalculate size based off new width
    imageSize = (text as NSString).boundingRectWithSize(CGSizeMake(currentW
idth, CGFloat.max), options: options, attributes: textAttributes, context:
nil)

    // Recalculate width:height ratio
    currentHeight = imageSize.height
    let currentRatio = currentWidth/currentHeight

    // If last change didn't improve, revert and give up
    if abs(ratio-lastRatio) < abs(ratio-currentRatio) {
        currentWidth = (lastDelta == InfinitweetDelta.Positive) ?
currentWidth - delta : currentWidth + delta
        imageSize = (text as NSString).boundingRectWithSize(CGSizeMake(c
urrentWidth, CGFloat.max), options: options, attributes: textAttributes,
context: nil)
        currentHeight = imageSize.height
        break
    }

    // If we're already near our target, give up
    if abs(ratio-currentRatio) < 0.05 {
        break
    } else { // Else keep going
        lastRatio = currentRatio
    }
}
```

As described earlier, this loop will adjust the `currentWidth` and recalculate the
`imageSize` until the width to height ratio is either close to 2, we cannot make it any
closer, or we run out of cycles. Once we have approximated the ratio as best as
possible, we can base the size of our Infinitweet off of this. Replace the line:

```
// TODO: Get final Infinitweet size
```

with the following:

```
// Round sizes for Infinitweet
let minSize = (width : CGFloat(440), height : CGFloat(220))
let adjustedWidth  = max(CGFloat(ceilf(Float(currentWidth))), minSize.
width)
let adjustedHeight = max(CGFloat(ceilf(Float(currentHeight))), minSize.
height)
```

```
// Outer rect is overall image size, Inner rect contains text
let outerRect = CGRectMake(0, 0, adjustedWidth + 2*defaultPadding,
adjustedHeight + 2*defaultPadding)
let innerRect = CGRectMake(defaultPadding, defaultPadding, adjustedWidth,
adjustedHeight)
```

The first set of constants define the width and height our Infinitweet will have according to the most recently calculated currentWidth and currentHeight, unless they are smaller than the given minimum size (below which the text becomes harder to read). The second set of constants define the sizes we will use for our Infinitweet; outerRect is the overall size of the image, whereas innerRect defines the bounds the text will occupy.

Once we know what size we want the image to be, the next step is to actually create a canvas using UIGraphics. After the canvas is created, we can draw the text onto it, export it as a UIImage, and store it in the self.image variable. To complete the Infinitweet algorithm, replace the line:

```
// TODO: Generate image
```

with the following lines of code:

```
// Generate image
UIGraphicsBeginImageContextWithOptions(outerRect.size, true, 0.0)
var image = UIGraphicsGetImageFromCurrentImageContext()

image.drawInRect(CGRectMake(0,0,outerRect.size.width,outerRect.size.
height))

// Set Background Color
defaultBackground.set()

// Fill background
CGContextFillRect(UIGraphicsGetCurrentContext(), outerRect)

// Draw text
text.drawInRect(CGRectIntegral(innerRect), withAttributes: textAttributes)

// Save new image
self.image = UIGraphicsGetImageFromCurrentImageContext()
UIGraphicsEndImageContext()
```

These will create a canvas for Infinitweet. For any given text string, we can now generate an Infinitweet. The next step is to integrate this into our app. Navigate to the PreviewController and replace the line:

```
var infinitweet = nil
```

with the line:

```
let infinitweet = Infinitweet(text: text)
```

With the exception of our remaining TODOs, this completes the bulk of the Infinitweet app for the Apple Watch. If you build and run the app at this point, assuming you have a synced Twitter account, it should work. However, there is still work to be done to let the user know when the app works and when it doesn't. We will cover that in the next section.

Providing User Feedback

Now that we have completed most of the behind-the-scenes work, our next step is providing the user helpful feedback: success messages when things go right, error messages when things go wrong. While on the iPhone or iPad you might be able to rely on UIAlertControllers to do the heavy lifting, the Apple Watch has no such equivalent in watchOS 1.x, though support is introduced in watchOS 2. As a stop-gap solution, we will have to create our own controller to handle the situation.

Navigate again to our Storyboard, and drag in a fourth Interface Controller. Under the Attributes Inspector, change the identifier of this controller to AlertViewController, so we can reference it as such from the code later. To this controller, let's first drag in a Group. Groups are typically used for containing certain portions of the layout on your app, but in our case, we will use it to change the background of the alert to let the user know whether or not the alert is good, bad, or something else. Change the Group's Height attribute to Relative to Container. It should now take up the whole controller, with the exception of the time. Additionally, change the Radius attribute value to 0. This will get rid of the rounded corners of the group.

Now, drag a Label into the Group. Again under the Attributes Inspector, change the Horizontal and Vertical attributes to Center, and make the Text Alignment centered. Finally, change the Lines attribute to 0, so it can fit any text we want to display. When complete, the controller should be similar to Figure 6.13.

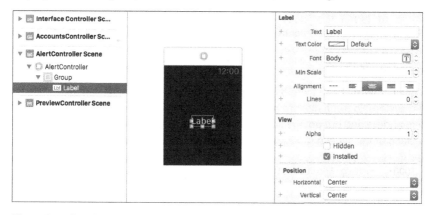

Figure 6.13. Completed AlertController

Now that our Storyboard is ready, we need to create another WKInterfaceController subclass to wire it to. Complete the usual steps for doing this, and name this controller AlertController. Then, navigate back to Storyboard and under Identity Inspector, set the class to our newly created AlertController class. Open the AlertController.Swift file in a new window, and control-drag from storyboard to the AlertController class to create IBOutlets for both the Group and the `Label` like we have done before. Let's uncreatively call the `WKInterfaceLabel` label, and the `WKInterfaceGroup group`. We've wired up our last Interface Controller!

Within the `awakeWithContext` method, add in the following code:

```
if context != nil {
    if let text = context!.stringForKey("alert") {
        label.setText(text)
        let positive = context!.boolForKey("positive")

        if positive {
            group.setBackgroundColor(UIColor.greenColor())
        } else {
            group.setBackgroundColor(UIColor.redColor())
        }
    }
    // TODO: Dismiss controller after interval
}
```

Breaking it down, if we passed a context dictionary with a `String` variable, `text`, this code will set the label's text to be that `String`. Then, depending on whether we receive a truthy value for a `Boolean`, `positive`, we decide whether to make the `Group` background green, for good, or red, for bad.

Now that we can show a message, the next step is to make it disappear after a given time interval. At the end of your `AlertController` class, add the following code:

```
func delay(delay:Double, closure:()->()) {
    dispatch_after(
        dispatch_time(
            DISPATCH_TIME_NOW,
            Int64(delay * Double(NSEC_PER_SEC))
        ),
        dispatch_get_main_queue(), closure)
}
```

This is a helper function I wrote that uses Grand Central Dispatch, Apple's threading system, to run a closure after a given number of seconds. It is simple enough to understand but going into detail is outside of the scope of this walkthrough. Now, in place of the `TODO` in the `awakeWithContext` method, add the following code:

```
delay(1, { () -> () in
    // TODO: Perform Additional Steps
    self.dismissController()
})
```

This will delay 1 second and then dismiss our `AlertController`. However, before we dismiss the `AlertController`, we may in some cases want to do other behaviors like returning to the app's home screen. In order to accomplish this, we need to create a delegate for the `AlertController`. At the top of the class, define the following delegate protocol:

```
protocol AlertControllerDelegate {
    func alertControllerDidCompleteDestructively(destructively : Bool)
}
```

This allows us to have our `AlertControllerDelegate` specify what actions we want to exhibit once we are ready to dismiss the `AlertController`. We will use the parameter `destructively` to tell us whether we want to return to the root controller after completion. Now, replace the new TODO in `awakeWithContext` with the following:

```
let delegate = context!["delegate"] as? AlertControllerDelegate
let destructively = context!["destructive"] as? Bool
if delegate != nil && destructively != nil {
    delegate!.alertControllerDidCompleteDestructively(destructively!)
}
```

This grabs the delegate passed in the `context` dictionary and then runs its delegate method, before proceeding to dismiss the `AlertController`. With this, we are ready to use our new `AlertController`!

Navigate to the `PreviewController`. First, make the `PreviewController` a `AlertControllerDelegate` by changing the class definition to the following:

```
class PreviewController: WKInterfaceController, AccountSelectionDelegate,
AlertControllerDelegate {
```

Then, in the `postImageToAccount` method, replace the line:

```
// TODO: We succeeded!
```

with the line:

```
self.presentControllerWithName("AlertController", context: ["delegate" :
self, "text" : "Success!", "positive" : true, "destructive" : true])
```

This will summon the `AlertController`, make it green, and display the text "Success!" when we've successfully posted the Infinitweet to Twitter. Let's do something similar for the error TODO below. Replace it with:

```
self.presentControllerWithName("AlertController", context: ["delegate" :
self, "text" : "Error", "positive" : false, "destructive" : true])
```

This will make a red `AlertController` with the text "Error" whenever we get an error trying to post. Now, in the `share` method, replace the line:

```
// TODO: No Twitter accounts synced by user
```

with the line:

```
self.presentControllerWithName("AlertController", context: ["delegate" :
self, "text" : "No Twitter Accounts", "positive" : false, "destructive" :
true])
```

This will alert the user saying "No Twitter Accounts" if they do not have any accounts synced to their device. Finally, replace the last TODO in the `share` method with the line:

```
self.presentControllerWithName("AlertController", context: ["delegate" :
self, "text" : "Access Denied", "positive" : false, "destructive" : true])
```

This notifies if they denied us access to their Twitter accounts for whatever reason. That's it! We should now be able to successfully build, run, and post Infinitweets from the Infinitweet Apple Watch app.

Finishing Touches

Now that we have a working Infinitweet Apple Watch app, we should clean up a few details. Right now, our app requires user approval from their iPhone before we can use their Twitter account. There is no way around this, but we can do a better job of letting the user know this is going to happen.

Navigate to our `PreviewController` class. In order to let the user know we need their approval, we need to check if we have the user's permission to post to their account. To do this, we need to remember when we get the user's approval using `NSUserDefaults`. If we do, then we proceed to pick an account to post from. If we don't, then we notify the user to check their iOS device, request approval, and remember we've gotten the approval if it is granted. In this case will pass the AlertController a false value for "destructive," indicating that we should wait for the user to handle this rather than exiting the current Infinitweet creation process. Replace all of the code in our `share` method with the following:

```
// Load Synced Account Database
let accountStore = ACAccountStore()

// Specify Type of Account we want to use
let accountType = accountStore.
accountTypeWithAccountTypeIdentifier(ACAccountTypeIdentifierTwitter)

// Check if we already have permission
var defaults = NSUserDefaults.standardUserDefaults()
if defaults.boolForKey("permissionsGranted") {
    chooseAccount(accountType, fromStore: accountStore)
} else {
    // Ask User to Check Device
    self.presentControllerWithName("AlertController", context: ["delegate"
: self, "text" : "See iOS Device", "positive" : false, "destructive" :
false])

    // Prompt user for permission to use their Twitter account
    accountStore.requestAccessToAccountsWithType(accountType, options: nil)
{
        granted, error in

        if granted {
            // Check if we have the user's permission
            defaults.setBool(true, forKey: "permissionsGranted")
            defaults.synchronize()

            self.chooseAccount(accountType, fromStore: accountStore)
        } else {
            self.presentControllerWithName("AlertController", context:
["delegate" : self, "text" : "Access Denied", "positive" : false,
"destructive" : true])
        }
    }
}
```

Most of the logic here is the same, except now we check NSUserDefaults in order to find out whether we have the user's permission to post.

> **Note**   Though in this case we use the standardUserDefaults, we could alternatively define a set of user defaults that could be shared across all user devices. We can do this using an iOS feature called App Groups, which among other things, allows us to share settings between different portions of the app (such as the iPhone, the Watch, and other extensions). Because we are not developing a full iPhone companion app, this is outside of the scope of this tutorial, but it is a good thing to keep in mind.

Additionally, we have also abstracted the account selection process into another function, which we will define after share:

```
// Choose account to post from
func chooseAccount(type : ACAccountType, fromStore store : ACAccountStore)
{
    let twitterAccounts = store.accountsWithAccountType(type)

    if twitterAccounts.count == 0 {
        self.presentControllerWithName("AlertController", context:
["delegate" : self, "text" : "No Twitter Accounts", "positive" : false,
"destructive" : true])
    } else if twitterAccounts.count > 1 {
        self.presentControllerWithName("AccountsController", context:
["accounts": twitterAccounts, "delegate" : self])
    } else {
        self.postImageToAccount(twitterAccounts.first as! ACAccount)
    }
}
```

You will recognize all of this code as the logic for selecting a Twitter account to post from (or presenting the AccountsController if we need the user to decide) that we wrote earlier. With these two changes, we will now have told the user to check their device for permission approval, and have removed our last TODO!

Additional Notes

Our Infinitweet app's code is now finished. However, that does not mean the app is complete; though this walkthrough exercise ends here, there is still plenty of room for improvement. Ideally, we would also create an iOS interface for users to send Infinitweets, allowing for much more room for customization when they do. This would also open up the road for more communication between the iPhone and Apple Watch app; sharing user preferences like default font settings and colors are all possible using App Groups, which we briefly described above.

Additionally, before this app is App Store ready, we would also need to give the UI more polish—improved font choices where necessary, ensure our color schemes are consistent, as well as add assets to our app—things like app icons and other images we may want to use in place of text. All of these are important to creating a beautiful app that encourages users to return.

As you have seen, Apple Watch apps have a number of limitations compared to iOS apps. These limitations have helped us along the way by simplifying the number of options we have available to us, but they also meant we had to improvise replacements for things like `UIAlertControllers` and Share Sheets. We have also seen that all of the behind-the-scenes action for Apple Watch apps takes place on the iPhone, not the Watch itself.

As you go forward building your own Apple Watch apps, always keep in mind simplicity, ease of use, and unobtrusiveness. Though apps on desktop or even mobile platforms aim to increase the amount of time a user is using their app, Apple Watch apps have the opposite aim: get a user in and out as fast as possible, and give them a sense of accomplishment for using your app. Following these principles will ensure not only that your users are pleased, but also that they keep returning to use your app.

Chapter 7

Developing Apple Watch Cross-Platform Apps

By Mark Griffin, creator of the FAIRFX Watch app

When smart phones became common place just a few years ago, there weren't many options when making applications for them. You could write code native to the device itself, whether that was Objective-C for iOS or Java for Android. As the platforms matured, more options became available to developers. One option was that developers could write code in a different language of their choice, and another option was the ability to export their code to multiple platforms.

With the advent of wearable technology, we've moved a bit back into the past when it comes to developing for these new platforms. Developers are required to build applications in whatever language is native for the new platform. This presents a challenge to those of us who are using one of the alternative tools. We might not have experience using the native languages, we might already have an application built to take advantage of cross-platform code, or we might prefer a different tool as personal preference.

This chapter will be helpful if you are not using native tools to link between your non-native application and the native tools of the wearable application. By building a cross-platform application we will look at how to communicate between native and hybrid code, and how to embed the native application into our project.

Our application will be built in Ionic and Cordova, which is a way of building applications using HTML that comes with its own set of native feeling components, however this section should keep it fairly easy for users of other platforms to follow along with little changes to the plugin and native code to adapt it for their needs.

Our application is pretty simple. It loads a data feed of currency rates and allows users to customize the base currency so they can see rates specific to them. They are able to make changes on either the Watch or their phone and the change will be reflected back on the other platform. Although this is a simple application, it will give you many of the tools you need to make a far more complicated application using the same techniques and expanding on the methods used to handle more complex interactions.

Even if your platform is different to the one we are using for this chapter, I suggest you follow along first with the guide so that you can be familiar with how and why the different elements interact together, which should then give you an understanding of how to approach your own issues. We will also outline many of the problems and pitfalls that might be presented along the way.

The FAIRFX Watch Application

FAIRFX is an international payment services provider, offering services to over half a million customers in the UK since 2007. The Group has developed a cloud-based peer-to-peer payments platform that enables personal and business customers to make easy, low-cost multi-currency payments in a broad range of currencies and countries and across a range of FX products via one integrated system. The FAIRFX platform facilitates payments either direct to bank accounts, or at over 30 million merchants and over 30 million ATMs in a broad range of countries globally via mobile applications, the Internet, SMS, wire transfer, and MasterCard/VISA debit cards.

I lead the mobile team at FAIRFX where I'm responsible for the application portfolio and ownership of mobile technical delivery, line managing the mobile engineering team, and ensuring an excellent customer experience across tablets to phones to wearable devices that enable our customers to manage their travel money. I want to ensure that a perfect union of the visible and invisible details of our services arrives seamlessly in the right place at the right time across all devices. Securely, discreetly, and intuitively. My intention is to show you how the FAIRFX mobile and Watch offering works by building both an iOS application and a WatchKit app.

The main FAIRFX mobile application is built in Cordova and the key features are allowing customers to top-up their travel card balance and transfer money to other bank accounts abroad. The application currently has a user base of over 50,000 customers (see Figure 7.1).

We recently launched an Apple Watch application to go along side the mobile application, which can help our customers have instant access to our services notably viewing transfer rates at a glance, as well as having up to the minute data on their wrist about their card balances. As part of our roadmap, we plan to develop a system of alerts and notifications to tell our customers when rates or balances change.

Figure 7.1. *Screenshots of the FAIRFX Application*

Building Watch Applications as a Cross-Platform Developer

The standard way to make an application for iOS devices is to use Apple's own Xcode along with either Objective-C or Swift, however many developers are taking to using other tools to make their apps. There are many reasons to do so. Some prefer a different language such as Xamarin offering C#, some prefer an interface that makes a particular task easier, such as Unity3D, and some people like to bring their applications to multiple platforms easily using something like Cordova.

The Apple Watch has been a very exciting addition for developers because it could be the device that pushes wearable technology into the mainstream. The good news is that the Apple Watch is relatively simple for a native Apple developer to pick up. But for those who are more familiar with some of these other tools opening up Xcode and trying to get something going can be challenging in multiple ways, such as not knowing the language, being unfamiliar with how the tooling works together, or just communicating between their main application and the Watch application.

Almost all of the tools mentioned allow you to create your own plugins to run native code directly from your main application so in this section we are going to look at how you can create a Watch application with little to no knowledge of the native tools. To do this we are going to be using Ionic as our tool of choice, but the methods used should be fairly similar between other platforms.

Building Our Main Application with Cordova

Our first step is to create a simple application setup that we can add our Watch application to further down the line. As previously mentioned, we're going to use Ionic to do this, which is a framework for creating mobile applications with HTML5. The first thing you'll need to do is install Node.js, which will provide us with the npm package manager. You can download and install it from here (https://nodejs.org/).

Once that is all set up, we need to go about installing Ionic. We can do this from the terminal by running the following.

```
sudo npm install -g cordova ionic
```

Our next step is to create the project. For this we are going to use a blank template and name our application watchDemo.

```
ionic start watchDemo blank
```

This will create a selection of starter files for you, which will contain your web application. I do not want to spend too much on this part of the application because you most likely already have your own application. For the purpose of this guide, we are going to create a very simple application, which loads the latest exchange rates from some json and lists them out so that we have a basic application to interact with our example Watch application.

Our first step should be to make sure everything is setup correctly, so let us run our blank application via a web browser.

```
cd watchDemo
    ionic serve
```

This should have opened a web browser with Ionic Blank Starter in a header bar and not much else. Let us get started with adding a template for our loaded feed. Grab the code editor of your choice and open up watchDemo/www/index.html. You can change the page title here if you feel like it.

First, we are going to create a template for us to load a select set of data into. Find the ion-content tag and insert the following.

```
<ion-item ng-repeat="rate in rates">
    1 {{base}} = {{rate.amount}} {{rate.rate}}
</ion-item>
```

We also need to add a controller to load and manipulate the data. You need to change the ion-content tag so it reads:

```
<ion-content ng-controller="AppControl">
```

Next we are going to get our application loading data. At first we will do this statically but we can move to a dynamic feed further down the line. Open up the file watchApp/www/js/app.js. Within the basic application, this contains all of the code to control our application, now let us add our controller. At the end of the file add the following in Listing 7.1.

Listing 7.1. Loading data

```
.controller("AppControl", function($scope) {
    var json = {
        "EUR": {
            "AUD":1.4338,
            "CAD":1.365,
            "GBP":0.719,
```

```
            "USD":1.097
        }
    };
    $scope.base = "EUR";
    var rates = [];
    var choice = json[$scope.base];
    for(var s in choice) {
        rates.push({
            rate: s,
            amount: choice[s]
        });
    }
    $scope.rates = rates;
} )
```

I'm not going to go into too much detail for this code because this book is about Apple Watch development and we are just building a quick application for us to work with, but hopefully it's simple enough to follow on. If you now run this code, as when you first tested the project, you should see a list of exchange rates (see Figure 5-2).

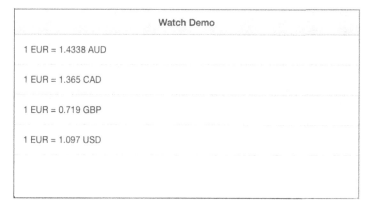

Figure 7.2. Exchange rates in our sample app

JSON does not tend to be too useful when it is embedded directly into the app, so let us both expand the data we are using and load the data remotely. In a real application you would likely have some server side logic to generate your JSON feeds, but for our purposes please copy Listing 7.2 below into a text file and upload it to some web space somewhere. We are naming ours rates.json.

Listing 7.2. Text file for our app

```
{
    "AUD": {
        "CAD":0.952,
        "EUR":0.6974,
        "GBP":0.5015,
        "USD":0.7651
    },
```

```
    "CAD": {
        "AUD":1.0504,
        "EUR":0.7326,
        "GBP":0.5267,
        "USD":0.8037
    },
    "EUR": {
        "AUD":1.4338,
        "CAD":1.365,
        "GBP":0.719,
        "USD":1.097
    },
    "GBP": {
        "AUD":1.9942,
        "CAD":1.8985,
        "EUR":1.3908,
        "USD":1.5257
    },
    "USD": {
        "AUD":1.307,
        "CAD":1.2443,
        "EUR":0.9116,
        "GBP":0.6554
    }
}
```

Now let us change the application so that it uses this data instead of the static JSON. The Ionic way to do this is by using a service. To do this, enter the following just after the closing bracket of the controller. I'm just loading the local JSON file here, but remember to change the path to wherever you uploaded your file.

```
.factory('RatesService', function($http) {
    return $http.get('rates.json');
})
```

Back in the controller we can now access this data by calling the getRates function of the RatesService. We are going to modify our controller a little so that the loading of data and processing of it are in their own functions. Here we are watching for any changes to the value $scope.json. When it changes we run the same processing code we were using before.

Listing 7.3. Wathcing for $scope.json changes

```
.controller("AppControl", function($scope, RatesService) {
    $scope.base = "EUR";
    $scope.$watch('json', function() {
        if($scope.json != undefined) $scope.updateRates();
    });

    $scope.loadRates = function() {
        RatesService.success(function(data) {
            $scope.json = data;
        });
    }
```

```
$scope.updateRates = function() {
    var rates = [];
    var choice = $scope.json[$scope.base];
    for(var s in choice) {
        rates.push({
            rate: s,
            amount: choice[s]
        });
    }
    $scope.rates = rates;
}

$scope.loadRates();
})
```

Our final step before moving on to the Watch application is to export and build this project for iOS. Before doing this, now is a good time to set up the config settings for your project. You can do this by editing config.xml in the root of the project. In here you should customize the application id within the widget section. There are various other options that you can have a poke around in here with too. You should have something roughly like what is shown in Listing 7.4.

Listing 7.4. Editing config.xml

```
<?xml version="1.0" encoding="UTF-8" standalone="yes"?>
<widget id="com.fairfx.watchdemo" version="1.0" xmlns="http://www.w3.org/
ns/widgets" xmlns:cdv="http://cordova.apache.org/ns/1.0">
  <name>watchDemo</name>
  <description>
        An Ionic Framework and Cordova project.
    </description>
  <author email="info@fairfx.com" href="http://fairfx.com/">
      Ionic Framework Team
    </author>
  <content src="index.html"/>
  <access origin="*"/>
  <preference name="webviewbounce" value="false"/>
  <preference name="UIWebViewBounce" value="false"/>
  <preference name="DisallowOverscroll" value="true"/>
  <preference name="android-minSdkVersion" value="16"/>
  <preference name="BackupWebStorage" value="none"/>
  <feature name="StatusBar">
    <param name="ios-package" value="CDVStatusBar" onload="true"/>
  </feature>
</widget>
```

Now we can create an export of our application so that it's ready for iOS. This will package everything up into an Xcode project, which we can then use for adding our WatchKit functionality. To do this, perform the following from the command line.

```
ionic platform add ios
ionic build
```

This will now go ahead and create an Xcode project for us in the following folder, watchDemo/platforms/ios. Open it up and it should look something like what is shown in Figure 7.3.

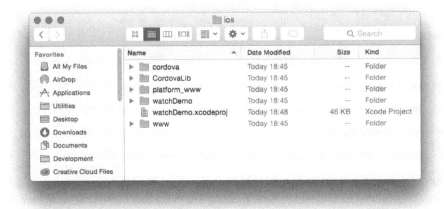

Figure 7.3. Exporting our app

Bridging the Gap

Now that we have our main application up and running, we can jump into making the Watch application more robust. At this stage, you could use the iOS project from earlier in this chapter and add a WatchKit target to it, but then you would have two stand-alone applications. What we really want to do is interact between our main application and the application on the watch, so first we are going to create some plugins that will enable us to do so.

First up, let's make sure everything is working with the iOS build. If you browse to the iOS folder you should find a file in there named WatchDemo.xcodeproj. Double-click this and it will open up with the Ionic application you made, ready to be exported to a phone or a tablet. Just to confirm that everything is working, tap the play button in the top left and you should have something similar to what you see in Figure 7.4.

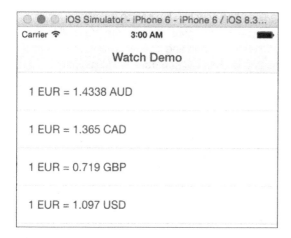

Figure 7.4. Our watch demo app

Jump back to your Xcode project now and expand the Classes folder. There should be a few other bits and pieces in here, but what we want to do is add a new Swift file. You can create your plugins in either Swift or Objective-C. For this demo I've decided to go with Swift because it shares more similarities with JavaScript, but feel free to use Objective-C. Things will be relatively similar, but you'll have to do some research as to what the alternative commands would be. Right-click the Classes folder, and select New File. Make sure iOS is selected on the left and that you are under Source, then select Swift File, as shown in Figure 7.5.

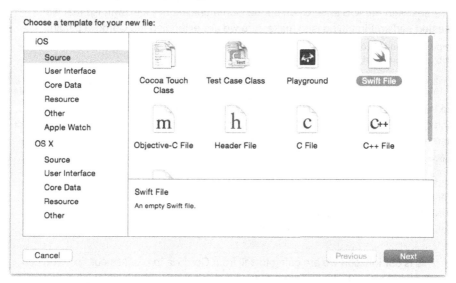

Figure 7.5. Selecting our Swift File

You will then get a dialog box for saving this new file. I'm calling mine CommincationPlugin. Type in the name you like and then click Create. You will then be asked if you'd like to configure an Objective-C bridging header. This is an essential item so make sure that you select Yes to this. This will generate two files, firstly the CommunicationPlugin.swift that we asked it to create, and also a WatchDemo-Bridging-Header.h, which was created to allow the main application to access the plugins code.

Our first step is to add the Cordova communication library, so open up your bridging header, which is WatchDemo-Bridging-Header.h and add the following.

```
#import <Cordova/CDVPlugin.h>
```

If you now try and build this project you should run into an error. By default, Ionic and Cordova were built for iOS 6. Swift only works with iOS 7 and above, and we are using some features that are only available in newer versions of iOS so we just need to change our settings slightly to make sure it'll work. Select the main project file within Xcode. It should be called WatchDemo. You should have a long list of settings broken down into different groups. We are looking for the Deployment Info group, and we want to change the Deployment Target from 6.0 to 8.0.

Once you've updated that variable, have a quick look down the project structure for CordovaLib.xcodeproj and carry out the same change there. This will be displayed in a different way, but you are looking for the variable iOS Deployment Target. To make it easier you can type that name into the search box at the top of this section and it will only show you options that will match. Change this to 8.0 and you're good to move on.

Let's start off just testing if we have all of the linkage working correctly. First up, let's deal with the iOS side. Open up the CommunicationPlugin.swift file that we created earlier. First thing is to make sure we are extending the Cordova plugin.

```
import Foundation
@objc(CommunicatePlugin) class Communicate : CDVPlugin {
}
```

The import Foundation line brings in the basic Swift functionality. The next line sets up the class for our plugin, extending CDVPlugin so that Cordova can find our code, and @objc(CommunicatePlugin) is how Objective-C and, in turn, Cordova will see the name of our plugin. The class Communicate is setting the internal Swift name of our class.

For our test function we are going to take a value sent from our main application, convert it to uppercase, and then send it back to our application to do with as we please. Go inside the class and enter the following.

```
func echo(command:CDVInvokedUrlCommand) {
}
```

This is our function we are going to call from Cordova to process our text. You can name it whatever you like and have many functions within this class for your application to communicate with. The CDVInvokedUrlCommand is the information we have sent from our main application. Let's add some code inside the newly created function.

```
var message = command.arguments[0] as! String
message = message.uppercaseString
```

```
var pluginResult = CDVPluginResult(status: CDVCommandStatus_OK,
messageAsString: message)
commandDelegate.sendPluginResult(pluginResult, callbackId:command.
callbackId)
```

Going through line by line, we first take the value passed into our function, command, and cast the first index of that property to a string. Next we take that string and convert it to uppercase. We then create our result object as a CDVPluginResult, passing in the converted string. Last, we use the commandDelegate to send the result back to Cordova.

Let's move over to the Cordova side. Just to test this code we'll put it in the $ionicPlatform.ready function to make sure all of Cordova and Ionic have loaded before trying to use the plugin. If you look at the top of app.js you should find the $ionicPlatform.ready function. After everything else is in the function, go ahead and put the following.

```
cordova.exec(function(val) {
    console.log('success: ' + val);
}, function() {
    console.log('fail');
}, "Communicate", "echo", ["Rates are loaded"]);
```

We start here by calling exec, or the main Cordova object. This is what looks for plugins. We then set up each of our success (which logs out the data we got back) and our failure functions. Next, we specify the name of the plugin we are using in our main application, Communicate, and which function to call Echo. Last, we send in our array of options.

Our final step to get this plugin up and running is to let Cordova know how our main application and our iOS app call our plugin. Open up plugins/ios.json and look for a bunch of elements, which start with <feature name=. We want to add our own one of these for our plugin. After the last of these elements, add the following.

```
,{
    "xml": "<feature name=\"Communicate\"><param name=\"ios-package\"
value=\"CommunicatePlugin\" /><param name=\"onload\" value=\"true\" /></
feature>",
    "count": 1
}
```

First note, remember to use a comma at the start as we are adding a new value to the array. Here we are specifying the names used by Cordova <feature name="Communicate"> and the name of the class used by iOS <param name="ios-package" value="CommunicatePlugin" />. It's worth noting that this section of XML should be included in your config.xml, and this plugin file should update from there but there is currently a bug with Ionic and it doesn't pick it up so we have to add it manually.

Save up, build your project for iOS again from the command line (Ionic build ios) and then jump back into Xcode and hit the play button. If all is going well, you should see the same application as before, but if you look at the output window you'll notice something similar to the following.

```
2015-06-01 03:50:01.305 watchDemo[4403:330267] success: RATES ARE LOADED
```

You can see that it has taken our string from JavaScript, sent it to iOS and converted it to an uppercase string via Swift before returning the result to our main application for the JavaScript to console.log out. Let's move on to using this plugin to save some data for our Watch application to read.

When running different applications on iOS they are all sandboxed into their own unique area so they can't affect anything else. This is even true for different targets embedded in the same application. This can make it complicated when trying to communicate back and forth between the Apple Watch and your main application. There is a way around this however, and that is called App Groups.

App Groups are a fairly recent feature in iOS, which allow you to share some data between any applications that belong to the same group. It requires a little bit of setup to do, which you'll need to jump over to Xcode for.

Select the main settings at the root of your project called WatchDemo. From here we need to make sure we have the Target selected as WatchDemo, and then we can select Capabilities along the top bar. Scroll down here until you find App Groups, and tap the on/off switch to enable the feature. Xcode will go off and check online for any App Groups you already have prompting for you to select the correct developer account. Once that is complete you can tap the little '+' icon just below the App Groups box (see Figure 7.6). You'll be prompted to enter a new container name here, the best approach is usual to use the same id as your main application, but start that name with Group. Click OK and your group should now be good to go.

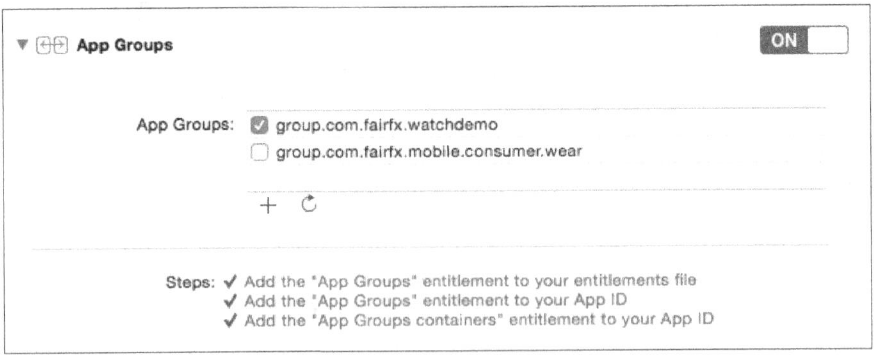

Figure 7.6. Sharing data with App Groups

With that set up, we can now look at saving and reading data. To do so we're going to create our own class, which we can use for both the Watch and the main application. Let's first create a new Swift file named CommunicateData.swift.

```
import Foundation
public class CommunicateData:NSObject {
    public static let groupID = "group.com.fairfx.watchdemo"
    public let data = NSUserDefaults(suiteName: groupID)
}
```

Here we are creating our Swift class, importing Foundation as usual. We have just used a plain name for the class name unlike last time because we don't need this code to be accessible from Objective-C. We next set our group id to be the same as the App Group ID we set earlier, and then we create our data object that we'll use for storing our data, which is an instance of NSUserDefaults.

```
    public var userCurrency:String {
        set {
            data?.setObject(newValue, forKey: "userCurrency")
            data?.synchronize()
        }
    }
```

The primary step is to save some data. We create a public variable called userCurrency, and in here we're going to store the most recent value the user selected within the main application as their currency (we'll add that actual functionality in a bit). To do this we then add a setter within the object, which takes the passed in newValue and assigns it to our userCurrency key. After this we then synchronize this data so that it's then accessible elsewhere. Add this next bit of code after the closing brace for the setter.

```
get {
    if data?.objectForKey(dataKey) == nil {
        data?.setObject("EU", forKey: dataKey)
        data?.synchronize()
    }
    return data?.objectForKey(dataKey) as! String
}
```

So here is the code for our getter. We first check if the key exists. If it does not, then we need to set it to a default. In this case, the default is Euros. We sychronize as before because we have had to update the data. Next we return whatever is in our key. The complete code should look like Listing 7.5.

Listing 7.5. Our getter code

```
import Foundation
public class CommunicateData:NSObject {
    public static let groupID = "group.com.fairfx.watchdemo"
    public let data = NSUserDefaults(suiteName: groupID)
    private let dataKey = "userCurrency"

    public var userCurrency:String {
        set {
            data?.setObject(newValue, forKey: dataKey)
            data?.synchronize()
        }
```

```
        get {
            if data?.objectForKey(dataKey) == nil {
                data?.setObject("EU", forKey: dataKey)
                data?.synchronize()
            }

            return data?.objectForKey(dataKey) as! String
        }
    }
}
```

Let's jump over to our CommunicatePlugin.swift class to hook everything up that is ready for adding to our application. You can keep the echo function here if you'd like, or get rid of it because we're unlikely to use it again. We're going to make two new functions, one for saving data and one for reading it. Let's start with reading.

```
func readCurrency(command:CDVInvokedUrlCommand) {
    var currencyData = CommunicateData()
    var currency = currencyData.userCurrency
    var pluginResult = CDVPluginResult(status: CDVCommandStatus_OK,
messageAsString: currency);
    commandDelegate.sendPluginResult(pluginResult, callbackId: command.
callbackId)
}
```

This should all be pretty simple based on the code we already had. We first create an instance of our CommunicateData class, we then grab whatever the value is of the userCurrency variable. Then, just like the echo function, we return that data via a CDVPluginResult to our main application.

```
func saveCurrency(command:CDVInvokedUrlCommand) {
    var currency = command.arguments[0] as! String
    var currencyData = CommunicateData()
    currencyData.userCurrency = currency;
    var pluginResult = CDVPluginResult(status: CDVCommandStatus_OK)
    commandDelegate.sendPluginResult(pluginResult, callbackId: command.
callbackId)
}
```

Our save function is very similar to the load, except we grab the passed in data first as a String and then set it to our userCurrency value in our CommunicateData class. Lastly we let our calling function know that everything went fine. Your CommunicatePlugin should look like this in full.

Listing 7.6. *The full CommunicatePlugin*

```
import Foundation
@objc(CommunicatePlugin) class Communicate : CDVPlugin {
    func readCurrency(command:CDVInvokedUrlCommand) {
        var currencyData = CommunicateData()
        var currency = currencyData.userCurrency
        var pluginResult = CDVPluginResult(status: CDVCommandStatus_OK,
messageAsString: currency);
        commandDelegate.sendPluginResult(pluginResult, callbackId: command.
callbackId)
```

```
    }
    func saveCurrency(command:CDVInvokedUrlCommand) {
        var currency = command.arguments[0] as! String
        var currencyData = CommunicateData()
        currencyData.userCurrency = currency;
        var pluginResult = CDVPluginResult(status: CDVCommandStatus_OK)
        commandDelegate.sendPluginResult(pluginResult, callbackId: command.
callbackId)
    }
}
```

Let's get this all hooked up to our main application. First open up the index.html file so we can add the ability to pick and change currencies. Locate the ion-item element and add the following to it after it's repeated.

```
ng-click="changeBase(rate.rate)"
```

Now let's jump back over to the app.js file to add some code to control this and some other business. First, we should remove our old call to the echo function within the opening run section. We also want to make sure that our main controller knows when the application has finished loading so we can check if there is any data in our plugin. At the top of the run function add $rootScope after $ionicPlatform. Then within the ready function set $rootScope.loadComplete to true. Your run function should read like this:

```
.run(function($ionicPlatform, $rootScope) {
  $ionicPlatform.ready(function() {
    if(window.cordova && window.cordova.plugins.Keyboard) {
      cordova.plugins.Keyboard.hideKeyboardAccessoryBar(true);
    }
    if(window.StatusBar) {
      StatusBar.styleDefault();
    }
    $rootScope.loadComplete = true;
  });
})
```

Next, let's add a watch for this loadComplete. To get set, first add $rootScope to our AppControl, then enter the following code.

```
var loadInterval = setInterval(function() {
    if($rootScope.loadComplete) {
    }
    clearInterval(loadInterval);
}, 500);
```

This will let us run some code only when the app has fully loaded. Let's first add some code to read our App Group object, within the if statement checking for the loadComplete to be set to true add the following.

```
try {
    cordova.exec($scope.currencyLoaded, function(){}, "Communicate",
"readCurrency", []);
} catch(e) {
    $scope.currencyLoaded("USD");
}
```

We've wrapped this code in a try/catch block to make sure when running in a browser or on a device without the plugin that we still have something to fall back to. This is very important with cross-platform applications because you need to think about what will happen to customers who are on a different platform to the extension you are making. You can either make a plugin specific to that platform as well, or you can just make sure you can handle instances where the plugin doesn't exist.

The code above calls our Communicate plugin and asks for the readCurrency function within there. We're passing an empty array because we don't have any data that we need to send. $scope.currencyLoaded is a function we will create in a moment and the second function here is used if cordova.exec fails. We're not using it here, but depending on what your plugin is doing, you might need to have some fallback code to handle any issues it might have with the results.

After the loadInterval we'll add the $scope.currencyLoaded function to handle the result from the previous function. This is pretty simple.

```
$scope.currencyLoaded = function(val) {
    $scope.base = val;
    $scope.loadRates();
}
```

This just changes the current base value in use and then calls our existing loadRates function to populate the data for our application. Lastly, we'll send some data back to our plugin so that we can save the currency value to the App Group and then read it both back in the application and in the Watch application. Add the following after the last function you made.

```
$scope.changeBase = function(newBase) {
    $scope.base = newBase;
    $scope.updateRates();
    try {
        cordova.exec($scope.currencyLoaded, function(){}, "Communicate",
"saveCurrency", [newBase]);
    } catch(e) {}
}
```

This is the code to handle when a user taps on one of the currency values. We take the currency type that was tapped and set it as the base value on our scope. We then call the updateRates function to reload the display with the new data. After this we call our saveCurrency function within the Communicate plugin, passing in the new base value.

If you save up, build, and then run the app in Xcode, you should get the rates for Euros at first (this is the default value from the plugin when nothing is set). If you tap a couple of fields and quit the application and reopen it, you should see it load with whatever the last value selected was. This is all loading the data from the App Group. This is the same data we'll use for loading data for the Watch. Here is the full code for the controller (in Listing 7.7).

Listing 7.7. *Our controller*

```
.controller("AppControl", function($scope, RatesService, $rootScope) {
    var loadInterval = setInterval(function() {
        if($rootScope.loadComplete) {
            try {
                cordova.exec($scope.currencyLoaded, function(){},
"Communicate", "readCurrency", []);
            } catch(e) {
                $scope.currencyLoaded("USD");
            }
            clearInterval(loadInterval);
        }
    }, 500);
    $scope.currencyLoaded = function(val) {
        $scope.base = val;
        $scope.loadRates();
    }
    $scope.changeBase = function(newBase) {
        $scope.base = newBase;
        $scope.updateRates();
        try {
            cordova.exec($scope.currencyLoaded, function(){},
"Communicate", "saveCurrency", [newBase]);
        } catch(e) {}
    }
    $scope.$watch('json', function() {
       if($scope.json != undefined) $scope.updateRates();
    });

    $scope.loadRates = function() {
        RatesService.success(function(data) {
            $scope.json = data;
        });
    }
    $scope.updateRates = function() {
        var rates = [];
        var choice = $scope.json[$scope.base];
        for(var s in choice) {
            rates.push({
                rate: s,
                amount: choice[s]
            });
        }
        $scope.rates = rates;
    }
})
```

Getting a WatchKit App Up and Running

Now we can get on to the part that most cross-platform developers dread, working with Xcode. Don't worry, it's not that bad; I promise. Let's now add our WatchKit target so we can begin some Watch development. To do this, in Xcode, go to File ➤ New ➤ Target. This will open a dialog box with quite a few options, which could be confusing to the non-native developer. We're not interested in most of what you see here. On the left hand side of the dialog box you have iOS and OS X main sections, then a number of sub-categories. Under the iOS section we want to select Apple Watch (see Figure 7.7). You should now only have one option on the right-hand side, which conveniently is the one we want, WatchKit App for watchOS 1. Make sure this is highlighted, and click Next.

Figure 7.7. Accessing our WatchKit app

The next screen lets us set up some options for our new target. You probably will not need to change too much within here. The main things to look at are the tick boxes just a little over half way down. These let you decide if you'd also like to include Notifications and Glance scenes along with your main application. For our demo application, we're just creating the main application, so leave both unchecked. When you're done, click Finish (see Figure 7.8).

Choose options for your new target:

Product Name:	watchDemo WatchKit App
Organization Name:	FAIRFX
Organization Identifier:	com.ionicframework.watchdemo271323
Bundle Identifier:	com.ionicframework.watchdemo271323.watch...
Language:	Swift
	☑ Include Notification Scene
	☐ Include Glance Scene
Project:	🖹 watchDemo
Embed in Application:	🅐 watchDemo

Cancel   Previous   **Finish**

Figure 7.8. Setting up options for our target

We are now set up to start developing a Watch application, which we can release along side our main application written in Cordova. Xcode has generated a couple of things for you, but first of all, let's test our newly set up WatchKit application to see what's been created for us already. Xcode should automatically set the WatchKit application as the build target, but just to make sure, you need to select it from a little drop-down menu just to the right of the Play and Stop buttons at the top left of the Xcode window. From here select WatchDemo WatchKit App, then tap on the Play button (see Figure 7.9).

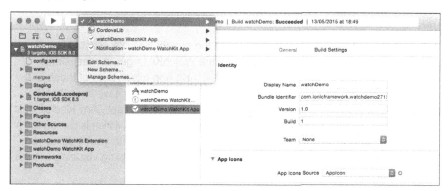

Figure 7.9. Running the WatchKit app

Most likely, not much will happen. If you are running Xcode 6, the iOS emulator doesn't actually launch the Apple Watch emulator part while testing a WatchKit application. To do this, make sure you have the emulator selected and go to Hardware

➤ External Displays ➤ Apple Watch (38mm). This should pop up a little companion window ready to emulate the Watch, but it will not be running anything (see Figure 7.10). Now you've got the window open go back to Xcode and press the Play button again. On newer versions of Xcode you should have the option to run the application with both an iOS device and a Watch.

Figure 7.10. Launching the Apple Watch simulator

A black screen isn't perhaps the most exciting thing, but you've now created your first WatchKit application. Let's go and add something just to show that it's fully working, then we can get on with making it more functional.

Jump back over to Xcode and take a look at the project files. You should have two folders that were created when you added the WatchKit target, a watchDemo WatchKit Extension folder and a watchDemo WatchKit App folder, both of these are required when making an application (see Figure 7.11). The way it works is that the App target contains everything that will be shown on the Watch itself. Any kind of logic and functionality will be carried out by the companion Extension, which is run on the phone. Data is then communicated via Bluetooth. For most of what you're doing you shouldn't have to worry about the two targets any more than knowing visuals go in the App folder, and logic goes in the Extension folder.

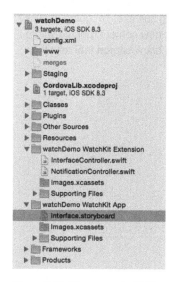

Figure 7.11. *The new project folders*

Let's add something visual and then jump into the App folder and click Interface. storyboard. This file is used to describe the different screens our WatchApp will have and how they link together. You should have two notification scenes and then the main scene called Interface Controller Scene. This is the one we're going to be working with for now.

Make sure you have all of the extra tools windows open in Xcode by clicking the icons at the top right. We specifically need the right-hand panel, which provides us with the different UI elements we can add to our Watch.

At the bottom of this right-hand panel, make sure the Object Library is selected, select the Label item (see Figure 7.12), and drag it over onto our Scene.

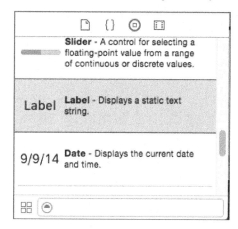

Figure 7.12. *Selecting the label for dragging*

Now double-click inside the window and type something suitable. I'm going to stick with Hello World. Clicking on Play again should show your new content running within the application and prove to you it can be more than just a blank screen that tells the time.

Figure 7.13. Our Hello World message is running

Let's tweak our Storyboard so we can use it to display rates much like in the application. Drag over a Table element from the Object Library. This will create a Table element with a Table Row Controller inside of it, and a Group inside of that. Inside of the Group, drag over a Label field again. Make sure this goes inside of the Group object.

Feel free to now tweak the Attributes inspector to align the text how you'd like it. I'm going to change the old Hello World text to say CUR, which we'll populate with information later. You should end up with something like what is shown in Figure 7.14.

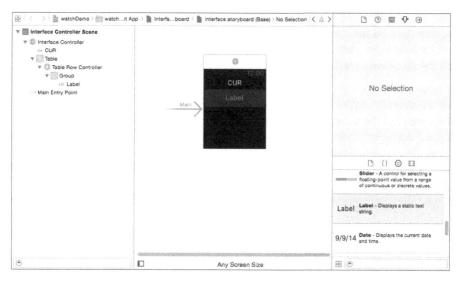

Figure 7.14. *We've added CUR as a label*

Next up, we need to find a way to code these elements. For this we should do a bit of prep first so there is something there to link to. The first thing we want to do is load some data, just like the main app does. We can connect to the same JSON feed we used before. There's always the option to save all of that data to the App Group we used before, but this would have the limitation that it was only as up to date as the last time we used the application, so we'll grab the files each time the user opens the application just to make sure we're using the latest data.

Loading JSON in Swift is a bit difficult. My personal recommendation is to use an open source library called SwiftyJSON. This makes working with XML much nicer and closer to how we worked with JSON in our main application. You can download SwiftyJSON from here.

```
https://github.com/SwiftyJSON/SwiftyJSON/blob/master/Source/SwiftyJSON.
swift
```

Download that file and drag it straight into you WatchKit Extension folder, and then select Finish for accepting the default options. Now we also want to add a class to manage each of our table cells. To do so, right-click the WatchKit Extension folder, select New File, and then select an iOS, Swift File. Name this CurrencyRowController. swift and tap create. We'll now drop in a basic class so we can see the controller when we do the linkage. Add the following to the file you just made.

```
import Foundation
import WatchKit
class CurrencyRowController: NSObject {
}
```

This is similar to the classes we've made before, but you'll notice that this time we've also imported the WatchKit libraries. Now we're all set to create our linkages.

Head back to the WatchKit App and open up the Interface.storyboard again. Select the Assistant Editior at the top right-hand corner of the screen. This should open the InterfaceController.swift file next to the Storyboard that you just opened. If not, then use the drop-down menus to browse to the correct file.

Now, using your right mouse button, drag the Label at the top of your storyboard to the inside of the WKInterfaceController class. It should show you a highlighted line when you're in the correct spot. Name it baseRate and tap Connect (see Figure 7.15). This will add some code for you to reference the element, and it will connect the item in your Storyboard to that variable. Now let's do the same with the Table element and name this one currencyTable.

Figure 7.15. Connecting the label to our WKInterfaceController class

Last, we want to link up our Label element with our CurrencyRowController class. To do this, first select the Currency Row Controller on our Storyboard, and select the Identity Inspector on the far right hand panel. At the top of this panel is a field for you to put the Class you want to use, so type CurrencyRowController. It should offer you an auto-complete if it recognizes the file. Next, change the tab to the Attributes Inspector and set the Identifier to be CurrencyRow. Now you can drag the Label element into the CurrencyRowController class and name it to labelText.

Let's move on to getting some data in. Open up InterfaceController.swift from the WatchKit Extension. You can return your view to the standard editor if you like in the top right. Create a function called loadData and put the following in:

```
let base = "AUD"
baseRate.setText(base)
let url = NSURL(string: "rates.json")
let task = NSURLSession.sharedSession().dataTaskWithURL(url!) {
    (data, response, error) in let json = JSON(data: data)
    self.currencyTable.setNumberOfRows(json[base].count, withRowType:
"CurrencyRow")
    var index = 0
    for(key: String, subJson: JSON) in json[base] {
        let row = self.currencyTable.rowControllerAtIndex(index++) as!
CurrencyRowController
```

```
        let amount = String(format: "%.4f", subJson.floatValue)
        println(amount + " " + key)
    }
}
task.resume()
```

Going through this quickly, we're first hardcoding the base value to AUD. We're then using that value to set the text of the label at the top of our display to show what currency is currently selected (see Figure 7.16). Our next step is to set the URL to our JSON file. Remember to set this to where ever you have your service or file uploaded. We create a task for loading the JSON and then parse that into a JSON object.

We set the number of rows based on the number of results we got back and told them to be an instance of our CurrencyRow object that we created earlier in the Storyboard. We then loop through all of the elements in the JSON result set, and print out the result. Lastly, we call the resume function on our task to actually set everything into gear. If you add a call to the loadData function from the willActivate one, you can run the application and start seeing a more productive application.

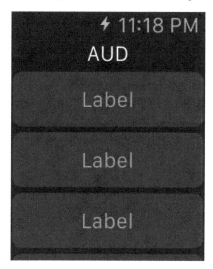

Figure 7.16. Hardcoding the base value of AUD

Let's finish this part off so we can hook our Watch application and our main application together. Jump over to the CurrencyRowController.swift file and within the setCurrency function we made earlier, add the following:

```
labelText.setText(amount + " " + base)
```

Now jump back over to our InterfaceController and call this function. Open up InterfaceController.swift and locate the following println(amount + " " + key). We can change this like the following.

```
row.setCurrency(key, amount: amount)
```

If you run the application again you should now get the values actually filled in.

Linking the Applications Together

Now that we have our applications up and running on both the phone and the Watch, let's look at linking them together. Our first step should be to take the value we saved into our App Group and to show and use it in the Apple Watch application.

First up, in our main Classes folder, select the CommunicateData.swift class that we made for our main application. In the panel on the right side find the section called Target Membership. Here you should click the tick box next to watchDemo WatchKit Extension so that the class is shared by both of our applications (see Figure 7.17).

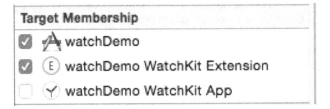

Figure 7.17. *Sharing our class with both apps*

We now also need to set up our WatchKit application to use the same App Group as the main application. Go to the watchDemo main settings file in the root of our project and make sure watchDemo WatchKit Extension is selected under Targets.

Now move over to Capabilities along the top tab and and find the App Groups section and expand it. Flick the little On/Off switch and you should be presented with a list of your available App Groups. Select the same one that we created before, and we can now jump back to our WatchKit Extension code.

Open the InterfaceController.swift and take a look down at our loadData function. We currently have a hard coded base value set. Let's edit this. Replace this code with the following.

```
var currencyData = CommunicateData()
var base = currencyData.userCurrency
```

If you run the WatchApp you will likely now see a different currency loaded to the one that was selected by default. If not, open the main application in the simulator and change the currency, then quit and reopen the Watch application (see Figure 7.18).

Figure 7.18. Our new currencies are now showing

Now we should look at going the other way. Allow a user to change the currency on their Watch and have that same change show up in the main application. To do this we need to tweak Storyboard a little bit, so go back to the WatchKit App folder and open the Interface.storyboard.

To add interaction we need a button, so drag a button component within the CurrencyRow object and select it. On the Attributes Inspector, change the Content from Text to Group and then drag our Label into the new Group that is created. Again, feel free to amend any positioning or layout you'd like to do.

If you run this you should get something that looks almost exactly the same as before, except if you tap one of the rates you should get a little depress animation showing that the elements are actually buttons now. Let's move on to linking them up. Go back to the Assistant Editor and make sure you still have the storyboard on one side and CurrencyRowController on the other, and then right drag your button object to somewhere within your code.

This one will be slightly different to the last linkages we've set up. This time change the Connection drop-down at the top to Action and name it updateRate. This will create a function that will run every time the button is clicked. We want to call our parent object instead in this case so we're going to add a delegate. At the top of the document after the public var base = "EU" code add the following variable.

```
weak var delegate: InterfaceController?
```

Now within the function we created, let's access this delegate. Your IBAction function should look like this.

```
@IBAction func updateRate() {
    delegate?.updateRate(base)
}
```

You'll likely get an error at first because we haven't created this new updateRate function on the parent. Open the InterfaceController and add the following function at the end.

```
func updateRate(base: String) {
    var currencyData = CommunicateData()
    currencyData.userCurrency = base
    loadData()
}
```

If you now run your code you should see that the Watch acts just like the main application and you can tap one of the rates and it will update to show the specific rates for that base. This is done by using our CommunicateData class to save the value to our AppGroup. This means if you now open your main application you'll notice it's also now showing the same data as the Watch application.

You should now able to go backwards and forwards between both the Watch and the main application with changes being reflected in both. This can be used for far more powerful information allowing a rich set of interactions to users.

Ideally you'd expand this application further so that when the App Group changes, the other applications will automatically read the new variable. The best way to do this would be to use a timer in both the JavaScript and on the Watch, but we will leave this as an exercise for the reader.

Common Pitfalls

Hopefully after following along you have both the application and the Watch application running well, however, during the process of trying to get things to play nicely between native and hybrid code I have encounterd various little issues. These problems can lead to you tearing your hair out until you find them. I'll try and outline a couple here to save you time in the future if you get stuck.

Different Version Numbers

One early pitfall is differing version numbers. All three targets that you are using need to be on the same version number. This can be confusing since earlier versions of Xcode used to let you have a different version number for the Watch application as well as your main application, but now you need to make sure they are all the same. This includes both the WatchKit Extension and the WatchKit application.

Differing Deployment Targets

Just because you're building for the Apple Watch, doesn't mean you are stuck with building your application for the latest devices. To hit the most users you should take into account what features your main application uses. If those are available with older deployment targets, you should drop it down. In our application, App Groups require a target of 8.0 while the WatchKit stuff is in 8.2. If we were to remove the App Group functionality, we could bring our target down to 7.0, targeting more users.

Downgrading the Deployment Target

At the time of writing, Apple Watch applications have to be set to deploy to a target of 8.2 and no higher. The latest version of Xcode however sets this value to be 8.3 by default. Luckily it throws an error but it can be quite confusing because you would assume it's due to something you've done.

Building Fine but Rejected at App Store

This is an issue that seems to mainly be related to Cordova applications. When adding the WatchKit application it seems that somewhere the Targeted Device Family can be reset to both the iPhone and the Apple Watch. This doesn't cause any issues when testing, but when submitting to the store you may get an error that your Watch application cannot be installed. This threw me for a long time because everything seemed to be correct.

To fix the issue you need to change the Targeted Device Family value for the Release version of the app. This should be set only to '4,' which represents the Apple Watch family. If you check your Build Settings tab of the WatchKit App you'll need to make this fix if the value is 1,4. Making the change can be fairly difficult because you can't edit the value within Xcode. The easiest way I have found is to get a finder window on your project. Right-click the xcodeproj file and select Show Package Contents. You can then open the project.pbxproj in any text editior and find the Targeted Device Family value there (see Figure 7.19).

▼ Targeted Device Family	<Multiple values> ◇
Debug	4 ◇
No condition allowed	1,4 ◇
Release	4 ◇
No condition allowed	1,4 ◇

Figure 7.19. Displaying the Targeted Device Family value

So now we have our application up and running on both the phone and the Watch. We have data communicating back and forth between both devices and hopefully it's given you an idea about how you can now go further and add more complicated interactions using the same techniques we have used here.

Additional Features

There are many other features available to you that we haven't covered so far in this chapter. Hopefully with your new understanding, it should be more approachable to you. The two main ones are Notifications and Glances.

Notifications

Notifications work much the same way as they do on an iOS device. The notification is fired off either locally or remotely and your phone will decide if the Watch should show that notification or not. Notifications come in two stages. The first is a brief message to let the user know something has happened. Second, if a user continues to look at the notification, it can expand into a more detailed message where a user can then act on the notification either directly from their Watch, or by opening the phone application.

Glances

Glances are relatively similar except they aren't prompted from a sent message. Instead, a user is able to look at a short piece of relavent data that your application provides. In our application for example, we could show their most popular currencies compared to each other. If a user decides to interact with a Glance, it will then take them through to the application.

Android Wear

As this section is about cross-platform development we should probably spend a little time thinking about what happens to your code when you are running on a different platform, and what you can do to offer your users a similar experience. The Android platform has their own alternative to the Apple Watch in Android Wear. While conceptually you can use the same techniques we have used in this chapter to create a plugin for Andorid, which could perform much of the same functionality, some of the ways Android Wear works is conceptually different.

Like you can now do with watchOS 2   (see the next section), Android Wear applications run on the watch itself. This allows apps to keep running even if the phone connection is lost, however, it adds some complications when trying to interact backwards or forwards between the watch and phone applications. This also causes an issue when trying to load remote data, because you have to send a request to the phone for the data, which will then load it for you and send it back.

Notifications also work a little differently with Android Wear. All notifications that are displayed on the phone are also sent to the Watch. You can customize these with additional information on your Watch and add different interactions for them to choose from.

Android Wear's other major feature is the ability to create custom watch faces, which at the time of writing Apple Watches do not allow. These can be very simple things or you can basically have a full application running, which gives the user a loads of extra information or animations.

WatchKit for watchOS 2

Shortly before the release of this book, Apple announced WatchKit for watchOS 2 with a few new features that have been added to Xcode 7. The good news is that all points raised in this chapter are still current and unchanged, but it does offer some alternative ways to work.

One of the key additions is that applications are now able to run on applications directly. When adding a target you can instead choose from the watchOS section and select a Watch application from there. This is good for applications that can be self contained and don't require too much interaction with the iOS device itself. The main feature that we were using, App Groups, are still fully compatible and would be my recommended method for communicating between the two different applications.

The other major addition to watchOS 2 is the introduction of ClockKit. While not fully giving the ability to make your own Watch faces, it does allow a degree of customization by allowing you to add bits of information known as Complications. For example, in our application we could show when a rate changes during the day. One of the nice features of this is that using the Digital Crown a user can scroll back in time through their Complications and see what happened and when.

Index

Get the eBook for only $5!

Why limit yourself?

Now you can take the weightless companion with you wherever you go and access your content on your PC, phone, tablet, or reader.

Since you've purchased this print book, we're happy to offer you the eBook in all 3 formats for just $5.

Convenient and fully searchable, the PDF version enables you to easily find and copy code—or perform examples by quickly toggling between instructions and applications. The MOBI format is ideal for your Kindle, while the ePUB can be utilized on a variety of mobile devices.

To learn more, go to www.apress.com/companion or contact support@apress.com.

Printed in the United States
By Bookmasters